DISCARDED TREASURES

A Biblical Defense of the Modern-Day Application of the Five-Fold Ministry and Gifts of the Spirit, and Why Today's Church has Largely Forsaken Them

ANDREW G. ROBBINS

authorHOUSE®

AuthorHouse™
1663 Liberty Drive
Bloomington, IN 47403
www.authorhouse.com
Phone: 833-262-8899

Published by AuthorHouse 04/04/2023

ISBN: 979-8-8230-0296-7 (sc)
ISBN: 979-8-8230-0308-7 (e)

Print information available on the last page.

Unless otherwise indicated, all Scripture quotations are
taken from the Berean Study Bible (BSB)
Copyright 2016, 2020 by Bible Hub
BibleHub.com

Scripture quotations marked ESV are taken from the English Standard Version
Copyright 2008 by Crossway

Scripture quotations marked BLB are taken from the Berean Literal Bible
Copyright 2021, Berean Literal Bible

Scripture quotations marked KJV are taken from the King James Bible, public domain

Terms and Word Usages in the Text

The word, *church*, with a lower-case c, refers to a local group of believers who worship together each week. *Church* with a capital C refers to the global body of Believers.

The word, *Gift*, with a capital G, always refers to a divinely inspired Spiritual Gift.

When the word, *Spirit*, appears with a capital S, it always refers to things associated with the Spirit of God. When *spirit* appears with a lower-case s, it relates either to the spirit of a person, the attitude in which he or she operates, or a demonic spirit.

The term *Five-Fold Ministry* is capitalized throughout the text by the author's preference to designate a category or grouping of ministry Gifts, which are also offices or roles in the Church for which people have been uniquely gifted. Thus, *Gifts*, *roles*, and *offices* are sometimes used interchangeably.

FOREWORD

BY DR. JERRY KING

The steps of a good man are ordered by the Lord...
-Psalm 37:23

It is extremely interesting to see how our Lord proves and illustrates this simple truth above in His Word.

For instance, a servant of the Lord is in a hotel gym trying to get much-needed exercise. His exercise machine of choice is reluctant to work properly, however, and the servant of God is not a skilled man with such devices. The man is about to give up on the workout and leave the facility to continue his journey to see his granddaughter, who is scheduled to graduate from West Point Military Academy, when another man "just happens by."

The second man, who has finished his own workout and is about to leave the facility, sees the first man's difficulties with the machine and offers to help. In no time, he has the machine functioning as the manufacturer designed it, and the helpful man begins to put his jacket back on to leave the facility when further conversation ensues. What began as a simple, embarrassed "thank you" turns into a three-hour conversation and then lunch.

This was the beginning of what was to become a God-ordered relationship; one that has continued through the years and is profitable for the Kingdom of God.

I have the privilege of being the first man identified as ineptly standing on what was, to me, a non-functioning machine and watching a perfect stranger walk up and in no time solve the mechanical problem with the exerting of obvious skill and little effort.

The second man introduced himself as Andrew Robbins (or Andy, as he prefers). He was relatively young, and I learned during breakfast on the second day that he was a pastor and had been seeking an older man with theological knowledge and experience who could become a mentor to him. I learned quickly that he and I shared a passion for God and the Church and came from similar backgrounds. And so, our friendship began.

It has been my pleasure to be a part of the journey of the man of God whose book you now hold in your hands. It has been equally gratifying to read this work, a treatise that is a concise and lucid treatment of subject matter vital to the Body of Christ. Too frequently, the subject matter dealt with here has served only to polarize the Church by emphasizing differences instead of clearly and respectfully stating biblical perspectives in a manner that can heal rather than further divide. Andrew Robbins, however, bends over backward in attempting to keep the unity of the Spirit through the bond of peace while dealing with issues on which not everyone is willing to dialogue.

In one of Jesus' departing statements to His disciples, He promised that the sending of the Holy Spirit would eclipse in value His continued presence in bodily form.

> *"...I tell you truth, it is expedient for you that I go away, for if I go not away, the Comforter [the Holy*

Spirit] will not come unto you; but if I go, I will send him unto you." -John 16:7 (KJV)

These statements, as Saint Paul would later deal with them in-depth, provide a proper understanding of the Holy Spirit's role in the lives of Christ followers. It was always the Father's intention that the many manifestations of the benefits of the Holy Spirit would become apparent in value to us through the centuries. This book illuminates those benefits and why we are unwise to minimize or ignore them.

At the time of this writing, I am 85 years old and have a personal library of hundreds of books I have read in my many decades of walking with the Lord. It is my judgment that you will find few examples of the intelligent and balanced treatment this author presents here on this subject for the consideration of the Church.

Jerry A. King, ThD
Preparing the Way Ministries

INTRODUCTION

In the spring of 1992, I returned to the feet of the Savior after a long prodigal journey. I was raised in church, but a dysfunctional family and a lot of resulting anger had led me to a place where I no longer wanted to meet the expectations of being a "good boy." God's hand was upon me, however, and He mercifully led me back to repentance at the age of 26.

Not too long after a fresh commitment to serve Christ, I found myself alone on a Friday night. My weekend nights typically had been filled with people and parties, but that evening I was alone, and this was a new and strange feeling for me. In the unfamiliar stillness, I felt the world's siren song beckoning me to make a call or two to see who I could hook up with to ease my intense feeling of loneliness.

At the same time, another voice was calling to me – a still, small voice. Thankfully, this was the voice I yielded to. Looking back, I believe that night was instrumental in setting the course of my life on a trajectory that would galvanize the Holy Spirit's firm grasp on my heart.

I did end up making a call or two after all, but it wasn't to hook up with a young lady or a party. I made some calls to find out if any church services were happening on a Friday night. There was one at the church I had abandoned when I set out on my prodigal journey, but it was a ladies' meeting. After thinking about it for a few moments, I decided to crash that ladies' meeting! I just *had* to be with the Lord's people. Something, or *Someone,* was drawing me.

After arriving late, I crept in and sat in the back row. But it wasn't a big church. The small room couldn't conceal me, and as the only male, I stood out. A woman was on the platform ministering to the group of ladies, a very energetic speaker with a prophetic anointing (I will define prophecy and other Spiritual Gifts in the following chapter). I intently listened as she preached, and after her teaching, she began ministering to people individually. That's when she spotted me.

The lady minister called me to the front of the room and began telling me details about my life only God and I knew – not private things that would embarrass me, but little things I hadn't told anyone. I knew God was speaking through this woman. As she continued to reveal the secrets of my heart, I broke down and sobbed as I felt God's mercy wash over me. It was as if He was saying, "It's okay, son. I've got you now. It's going to be alright." The lady minister then proceeded to tell me about my future, and I felt the comfort of God strengthen me.

It was a woman with a Spiritual Gift whom God used to bring comfort and strength to my heart. God made Himself known to me in a very personal and unique way.

From the beginning of my walk with Christ, I have had a strong commitment to daily prayer and in-depth study of God's Word. You will discover as you continue reading, in fact, how heavily I rely on the Scriptures, as I include dozens of Biblical references. But on that night in 1992, God would reveal His love for me through the exercise of a Spiritual Gift. This, too, is a way God speaks.

Fast forward twenty-five years. My family and I were on a summer tour of downtown Indianapolis taking in some of the monuments and historical sites. During our visit, my youngest son Drew, who was about ten years old at the time, was blessed by discovering a twenty-dollar bill lying on a step of one of the monuments. We looked around to see if anyone happened to be searching the steps for a lost bill but found no one. After a few moments, my wife and I gave the okay for Drew to claim the bill for his own.

That discarded treasure of the lost twenty-dollar bill reminds me of how the modern-day Body of Christ has treated the Five-Fold Ministry and Spiritual Gifts. Drew's happy discovery was likely the result of an adult who was careless with his or her treasure and lost it, only to have it discovered and claimed by a child. Similarly, most of the modern Church in the West has behaved as though there is little to no value in Spiritual Gifts and the Five-Fold Ministry, and has therefore carelessly discarded these treasures, leaving them for "less intelligent" people who seek after "emotionalism." As Jesus once prayed as recorded in Matthew 11:25,

> *"I praise you, Father, Lord of heaven and earth, because you have hidden these things from the wise and learned, and revealed them to little children."*

The deeper things of God's Kingdom are hidden from those who consider themselves "wise and learned" and are instead revealed to humble "little children."

In our intellectualized approach to heavenly things, much of the modern Western Church has rationalized away the imperative spiritual weaponry we will discuss in this book. Why is this? Perhaps it is because some of these concepts challenge our Western idea of sophistication. It could be fear of the unknown or losing control. Whatever the reason, we have settled for a sterilized form of Christianity neutered of power. This was prophesied over

2,000 years ago by the Holy Spirit through the Apostle Paul when he wrote,

> ¹*But understand this: In the last days terrible times will come.* ²*For men will be lovers of themselves...* ⁵*having a form of godliness but denying its power. Turn away from such as these!* -1 Timothy 3:1-2,5

Most Christians today have settled for a "form of godliness" that has little or no power. For many churchgoers, this is simply due to ignorance because they haven't been taught any different or seen anything better demonstrated.

In these last days, as the kingdom of darkness descends upon the earth like never before, we will have to face the fact that we cannot amble along in our Christian lives and survive without using the spiritual weaponry Jesus made available to us. We will have to utilize every tool and weapon at our disposal to fight the good fight of faith, building ourselves up in our most holy faith and setting captives free. Part of that armament is the Five-Fold Ministry and Spiritual Gifts.

What is the Five-Fold Ministry?

The "ministry" refers to all the service done to bring people into the Body of Christ (His Church) and to grow those in the Church to maturity in the Lord Jesus Christ. The Five-Fold Ministry Gifts are spiritual tools given by God to various individuals for building up the saints. The term "Five-Fold Ministry" has been coined in reference to a list of five ministry Gifts given by God to enrich His Church. The scriptural basis for this is Ephesians 4:11-13.

> ¹¹*And it was He [God] who gave some to be apostles, some to be prophets, some to be evangelists, and*

some to be pastors and teachers, ¹²to equip the saints for works of ministry and to build up the body of Christ, ¹³until we all reach unity in the faith and in the knowledge of the Son of God, as we mature to the full measure of the stature of Christ.

In summary, the Five-Fold Ministry is prophets, apostles, evangelists, pastors, and teachers. These Gifts also function as roles or offices in the Church for which people have been uniquely gifted by God for their application.

Today, a sect of Christianity teaches that the Five-Fold Ministry along with miracles and the Gifts of the Spirit all ceased with the first-century apostles. Those who hold this view have become known as "cessationists." On the other side of the aisle are those who contend that the Five-Fold Ministry, along with miracles and Gifts of the Spirit, are *continuing* today, and these have become known as "continuationists."

I have known several wonderful people who claim to be cessationists who I love and respect, and who I know love the Lord and are passionate about God's Kingdom. However, I'm afraid I must nevertheless respectfully disagree with cessationism, as these views are serious non-biblical errors which hinder the full expression of God's ministry in the Church. This is what inspires this writing. Still, while disagreeing on these peripheral issues, if we can agree on the centrality of our faith in Jesus as the Son of God Who died for our sins, raised on the third day and is the only way to reconciliation with the Father, we are brethren. Thus, we should heed Ephesians 4:3 in making **"every effort to keep the unity of the Spirit through the bond of peace."**

The fact that Christians divide themselves into camps over issues not even central to our faith is sad evidence we have not yet reached the full stature in Christ nor the unity in the faith described in Ephesians 4:11-13. This fundamental point alone disproves cessationism. I will elaborate on this as we proceed.

My purpose, therefore, is not to create further division, but by God's grace perhaps repair some of it since there is no small rift in some circles of the Body of Christ over the issues on which I will speak in this treatise. What we all want, hopefully, is to walk in Biblical truth, and if we can agree on that point, then it's possible to make some progress in unity.

In the Apostle Paul's discourse on Spiritual Gifts in First Corinthians chapters 12-14, he speaks to this unity in a brief statement at the end of chapter 12 verse 31.

The fact that Christians divide themselves into camps over issues not even central to our faith is sad evidence we have not yet reached the full stature in Christ nor the unity in the faith described in Ephesians 4:11-13. This fundamental point alone disproves cessationism.

But earnestly desire the higher gifts. And I will show you a still more excellent way. (ESV)

The excellent way he was speaking about is the way of love. This statement is the preface to what has become known as the famous "love chapter" in First Corinthians 13, where Paul goes on to say that a person can have knowledge, operate in Spiritual Gifts, and even possess faith to move mountains, but if the same individual does not have the love of God in motive and method, he or she is simply a noise maker. Unfortunately, we have a lot of noise makers on both sides of the aisle in the Body of Christ today who need to be more motivated by love.

I feel it is imperative that we get one thing straight in order for the balance of the book to be productive: *Those who have repented of their sins and turned to Jesus Christ as their Lord and Savior are all part of the same family.* As such, there should be no division among us even if we see certain peripheral doctrinal issues a bit differently. Genuine love and unity should be our chief aim even while trying to sort out the other marginal issues.

On that point, I do not claim to have a corner on truth with this treatise. After three decades of walking with the Lord, I am still growing and developing in my faith, just as I hope everyone reading this book is doing. The more I learn, the greater I realize there is so much I don't know. None of us have arrived at the place where we have everything perfectly figured out and no longer need to grapple with elements of our faith. The Scriptures tell us in Philippians 2:12 to work out our salvation with "fear and trembling," and that is how I am approaching this subject.

I pray this discussion will therefore move us toward the more excellent way of love and unity as we seek God's truth together and bear much fruit for the Kingdom.

1

DEFINING THE MINISTRY GIFTS

The Apostle Paul defined the role of each of the Five-Fold Ministry Gifts in Ephesians 4:11-13 as pointed out in the Introduction. Here we find the plum line for this discussion. Notice again each Gift or role as Paul describes them.

> *¹¹And it was He [God] who gave some to be apostles, some to be prophets, some to be evangelists, and some to be pastors and teachers, ¹²to equip the saints for works of ministry and to build up the body of Christ, ¹³until we all reach unity in the faith and in the knowledge of the Son of God, as we mature to the full measure of the stature of Christ.*

It behooves us to understand these Gifts more thoroughly and why God gave them to His Church.

The Pastor

Derived from the Greek word *poimen*, which means *shepherd*, the usage of *pastor* in the original Greek according to Strong's Concordance describes one who is a feeder, protector, and ruler of a flock of God's people. In the New Testament, we see this office in operation in the Apostle Paul's understudy, a young man by the name of Timothy with two epistles (letters to the churches) bearing his name.

I list this ministry Gift first not because it is necessarily the most important Five-Fold office, but because it is the most recognized in today's Church culture. It is a high-profile position, as the pastor is typically the "face" of a local church.

The pastor may have the most challenging of the Five-Fold Ministry roles in terms of relationships. Pastors guard, love, feed, nurture, encourage, protect, and care for the flock, yet it is not uncommon for pastors to be turned on and abandoned abruptly by the ones for whom they have poured out their lives. The Apostle Paul and his traveling companions found themselves in similar relational difficulties with some of the people in the churches they oversaw. Paul once lamented to the Corinthian church,

> **9For it seems to me that God has displayed us apostles at the end of the procession, like prisoners appointed for death. We have become a spectacle to the whole world, to angels as well as to men. 10We are fools for Christ, but you are wise in Christ! We are weak, but you are strong! You are honored, but we are dishonored... 12We work hard with our own hands. When we are vilified, we bless; when we are persecuted, we endure it; 13when we are slandered, we answer gently. Up to this moment we have become the scum of the earth, the refuse of the world. -1 Corinthians 4:9-13**

Paul's lament wasn't referring to only persecution from non-Christian people. Rather, he was referring also to the pushback he experienced from those in the church! Probably all pastors have experienced this same problem to some degree, at least the ones operating biblically and not watering down the message to tickle itching ears (see 2 Timothy 4:3). Pastoring is a very self-sacrificing role for that reason. Yet God calls certain people to lay down their lives for the sake of a sheepfold.

The Teacher

It is common for the pastor to also be well-versed in the ministry Gift of teaching, which leads to the next Five-Fold Gift. Teachers explain and clarify the truth, thus helping to ground the flock in the Word of God.

Please note that God has called *every* believer to mature in Christ and begin teaching others on some level according to Matthew 28:19 and Hebrews 5:12. But there is a gifting from heaven on certain individuals who are divinely skilled in this way. Teachers can take what others may see as complex subjects and make them simple, resulting in a strong foundation and deep roots in the Word of God for those in the church. While pastors are commonly also teachers, teachers aren't always pastors. In Acts 18:24-26, for example, we see three people mentioned named Apollos, Aquila, and Priscilla, none of whom were pastors, but all learned teachers and preachers of the gospel.

The Evangelist

Evangelists love sharing the gospel, and they are very effective at it! While every follower of Christ is called to share the gospel according to Mark 16:15, some are exceptionally gifted in this way. When they preach or share their faith, people get saved!

Phillip was known as an evangelist in the early church (Acts 21:8). While signs, wonders, and miracles often accompany their ministries, authenticating their message, this is not always the case.

For example, Billy Graham was a very effective evangelist who won millions of people to Christ with his crusades, but rarely did miracles happen at his meetings. Late German evangelist Reinhard Bonnke, on the other hand, won millions of people in Africa with his mass crusades, and miracles were commonplace.

The Prophet

The prophet guides and speaks on God's behalf under the guidance of the Holy Spirit. Prophets speak prophetically, meaning they often prophesy about future events as Agabus did in Acts 11:28 and 21:10-11.

The English term *prophet* comes from the Greek word *prophétés,* which means an interpreter or forth-teller of the divine will, according to Strong's Concordance. *Prophétés* is a compound word derived from two Greek terms: *pro,* meaning *beforehand,* and *phemi,* meaning asserting one idea over another, primarily through the spoken word. The Helps Word Studies says that a prophet (*prophétés*) declares the mind of God, which sometimes includes predicting the future.

The purpose of this Gift is to communicate God's will to people (Acts 13:1-3). Prophets also exhort and strengthen other believers (Acts 15:32). Prophets expose the secrets of people's hearts (1 Corinthians 14:24). A prophet also brings correction when necessary, as Nathan did with King David in Second Samuel 12.

Prophets are sometimes also referred to as "seers" in the Bible. A seer is a person who sees things revealed by the Spirit of God, which the prophet cannot know through any other means. This is often referred to as a "word of knowledge," and serves in part to bring validity to any prophetic words spoken later.

In the Introduction I provided the story of my first encounter with a prophetess who God used to comfort me when I was a babe in Christ. As another example of this type of genuine ministry in modern times, a different prophetess I had never previously met once picked me out of a crowd and gave me a word of knowledge. She said, "You will write a book teaching God's people the Biblical principles of finance." She could not have known I was already halfway through writing that book! Therefore, she got my attention right away, and I eagerly listened to what she had to say next. This exemplifies how prophecy and the "seer anointing" often function together.

On a side note, the Gift of prophecy is not gender specific as some may believe. Acts 21:8-9 tells us that the evangelist Philip had four virgin daughters who prophesied.

I must be quick to point out that there are undoubtedly satanic substitutes for the real thing regarding prophets. The description and biblical role of the prophet as presented here is quite different than those who practice magic arts with crystal balls, tarot cards, and other occultic practices which God strictly forbids and condemns (see Leviticus 20:6). It is also far removed from the self-proclaimed prophets that have dotted the religious landscape since ancient times. The false prophets of Baal and other pagan religions described in the Old Testament were so abhorrent to God that He commanded capital punishment for those who practiced such things. In the account of the prophet Elijah's confrontation with the worshipers of Baal in First Kings 18, 450 prophets of Baal were slaughtered on that day when God brought judgment against them. False prophets have been among us ever since. Familiar names would be people like Jim Jones, Muhammad, and Joseph Smith of the Mormon church, to name just a few. There have also been leaders in the Jehovah's Witness faith who have predicted a precise day of Jesus' return on more than one occasion only to be proven wrong when those days came and went.

In Old Testament days, prophets would be tested according to their track record of accuracy. However, on at least one occasion even a genuine prophet prophesied about judgment that ended up not happening, but this did not invalidate the individual as a prophet. For example, the prophet Jonah prophesied about the destruction of the ancient city of Ninevah and even proclaimed a specific time frame when the city would be overthrown, yet that judgment never came because the people of Ninevah repented, and God relented as a result. Did Jonah prophesy incorrectly? Was he a false prophet? No, he said exactly what God told him to say, but God simply changed His mind.

It seems common today for people to declare someone in ministry a "false prophet" who careens off into sin or false doctrine. On the contrary, some of these people were never prophets in the first place, so calling them false prophets misses the mark. Jim and Tammy Faye Bakker and Jimmy Swaggart are perhaps the most famous examples. Jimmy Swaggart functioned as a pastor and an evangelist, but he never claimed to be a prophet as described here. He never functioned in that role or ministry. Likewise with Jim and Tammy Faye Bakker. These were people who I believe genuinely loved God but who simply got off track and paid a high price. At the time of their downfalls, we could accurately describe them as backslidden, or in sin, or even preaching incorrect Bible doctrine perhaps, but they were not false prophets in the strictest biblical definition of that term. Jimmy Swaggart, by the way, is still in ministry today, albeit in a very different setting compared to his mammoth ministry of the 1980's when he admitted to sexual sin. He has had to pay high price for what he did, but he repented, and as a result God is still using him. God's grace is so wonderful!

I believe we need to be very careful about calling someone a false prophet, because similar to the situation described with Jonah, we may not know what God is up to behind the scenes. On the other hand, if someone has a long track record of inaccuracy or an individual makes declarations which clearly violate God's Word, that's different. We need to be discerning along these lines. But even genuine prophets are flawed people who can miss it occasionally. It should comfort us regarding our own shortcomings that the prophet Jonah literally rebelled against God's instructions, and even when he did carry them out, he did it through gritted teeth. Jonah's heart was not in a good place regarding his assignment to prophesy to a group of people he didn't like very much. Yet, in His amazing grace, God used him anyway.

The Apostle

An apostle is one who is sent and who governs. The term comes from the Greek word *apostolos*, which means *a messenger; one who is sent on a mission by a higher authority.*

Apostles preach the gospel in unreached regions and plant new churches (Romans 15:20), ordain people into the ministry (Titus 1:5), and disciple new converts until a pastor takes over (Acts 18:11). Throughout the book of Acts and the epistles we also see that apostles check up on churches to make sure they are healthy and growing in the Lord. Following the example of the Apostle Paul, who God sent to plant, raise up, and disciple various churches and act as an overseer to the pastor and elders, this is still going on today, of course, in the form of church planting and missionary work. Countless faithful missionaries plant numerous churches, nurture them to health, and provide ongoing support to the pastor.

An apostle can, at times, provide discipline to church members if necessary in matters where the pastor needs help or when the pastor himself needs correction. An apostle also refers to someone who is sent by God to proclaim a message, similar to that of an evangelist, but broader in the sense that it also involves church planting and overseeing, more akin to a missionary. The disciples of Jesus were later commissioned as apostles, but they were not the only ones, of course, as the ministries of Paul and Junia demonstrated.

The definition of apostle is so historically clear that even Wikipedia, a secular source, provides a clear and accurate description:

> "An **apostle** (/əˈpɒsəl/), in its literal sense, is an emissary; from ancient Greek literally 'one who is sent off', from the verb ἀποστέλλειν (apostéllein), 'to send off'. The purpose of such sending off is usually to convey a message, and thus 'messenger' is a common alternative translation; other common translations include 'ambassador' and 'envoy.' The term in Ancient Greek also has other related meanings.

> "... the term is also used to designate an important missionary of Christianity to a region, e.g. the 'apostle of Germany.' The word is used for those who were important in spreading his or her teachings."

This apostolic work is still going on today. Missionaries have been an important part of spreading the Gospel and establishing churches globally since the time of the first-century apostles. God's work continues through those called to be missionaries, or apostles.

Forsaking Not the Assembly

If God went to all the trouble to establish apostles, prophets, pastors, teachers, and evangelists to build up the saints, wouldn't it make sense to take advantage of these divine offices? Why would a Christian want to ignore or minimize that which God has established? And if God has provided an environment where these offices flourish called "church," wouldn't it make sense to faithfully attend an uncompromising Bible-preaching church where we can get fed, encouraged, challenged, and taught?

Apparently, even many Christians who *do* believe in the Five-Fold Ministry don't believe in the local church enough to be in attendance regularly, and this is to their harm. The King James version of Hebrews 10:25 tells us to "not forsake the assembling of yourselves together." The Berean Study Bible puts it like this:

> *24And let us consider how to spur one another on to love and good deeds. 25Let us not neglect meeting together, as some have made a habit, but let us encourage one another, and all the more as you see the Day approaching.* -Hebrews 10:24-25

It is much more challenging to spur one another to love and good deeds without fellowshipping with the saints in the environment of corporate worship. We are not to ease off the accelerator where church attendance and spiritual disciplines are concerned as we mature in Christ. This passage tells us we should be meeting together "all the more" in these last days, doing what the Apostle Paul told the Philippians when he wrote,

> *12I press on to take hold of that for which Christ Jesus took hold of me... 13Forgetting what is behind and straining toward what is ahead, 14I press on toward the goal to win the prize for which God has called me heavenward in Christ Jesus.* -Philippians 3:12-14

The Scriptures also tell us to make the most of every opportunity because the days are evil (see Ephesians 5:16). How can we make the most of every opportunity when we forfeit the easiest ones that present themselves on Sunday morning?

It is a deceived Christian who rationalizes his avoidance of church or inconsistent attendance. It is a prideful notion to believe you can thrive as a Christian in these evil days without being consistently connected to a solid local assembly. God placed churches and the divine offices accompanying them in place for a reason. They are for your benefit and mine. We ignore them to our peril.

> *It is in the environment of a church functioning biblically where access to the wonderful benefits of the Five-Fold Ministry and Spiritual Gifts are provided.*

I don't know a single Christian who attends church inconsistently who is flourishing spiritually or in his or her ministry. Not one. Effective ministry is tied to the local church, as is a big part of your spiritual growth. It is in the environment of a church functioning biblically where access to the wonderful benefits of the Five-Fold Ministry and Spiritual Gifts are provided.

I am not claiming it is impossible to grow spiritually without being part of a local church because God has provided many tools for our spiritual enrichment. We must recognize the magnitude daily fellowship with the Lord in prayer and study of His Word has in our spiritual progress and fruitfulness, for instance. And by taking counsel from the holy Scriptures, we learn that God has provided *many* tools for His children's spiritual growth and progress. Regular worship with the saints is part of that package.

We hinder our growth whenever we ignore even one of the various tools God has set in place for our spiritual development. If there is something we are not getting in terms of spiritual nourishment, we are not thriving to the extent we otherwise would. For example, a growing child cannot flourish by eating only beans and cornbread. He may get enough calories to keep from going hungry by eating those three times per day, but there is not enough broad-spectrum nutrition to cause his growing body to flourish like it otherwise would. As a result, he is going to be malnourished and may suffer health maladies.

Unfortunately, many modern churches do not emphasize every part of the Five-Fold Ministry and are therefore incomplete in providing all the tools available in God's Kingdom for the building up of the saints. Most churches at least have a pastor, and this by itself is good. However, there are other events and opportunities to seek out prophets, evangelists, apostles, and various teachers. There is no shortage of these types of ministries in this information age. You simply have to look around a little.

Of course, cessationist theology claims two of these offices have passed away. Against the instruction of First Thessalonians 5:20, which instructs us to "not treat prophecies with contempt," it is claimed that prophets and apostles are no longer operational, and the only valid offices are pastors, teachers, and evangelists. Some even go so far as to suggest that those of us who *do* believe in the modern application of these divine offices are not saved; that we are practicing some sort of pseudo-Christian mysticism. There are well-known ministers, in fact, who spend a significant portion of their pulpit time denouncing "charismaniacs" as heretics.

Why such an uproar? Why such vitriol? Are there any passages in the Bible suggesting people are damned who believe in the timeless nature of the Five-Fold Ministry and Gifts of the Spirit? Can a single verse be found even hinting at such a thing?

2

THE FIVE-FOLD MINISTRY CONTINUES TODAY

Cessationists contend that the Five-Fold Ministry passed away at the end of the first century because we have reached the "fullness," meaning the revelation from God to mankind was completed when the New Testament was canonized. There are several difficulties with this view.

The Proof of the Pudding is in the Eating

The old saying, "the proof of the pudding is in the eating," means you had to try the food to know if it was good or if you liked it. The saying has evolved and shortened to, "The proof is in the pudding." Its modern-day use means that to know if something is good or works, it must first be put to the test. Therefore, in keeping with this standard of putting something to the test in order to validate it, let's apply this to the Five-Fold Ministry.

First, we must consider the words of Romans 15:4:

> *For everything that was written in the past was written for our instruction, so that through*

endurance and the encouragement of the Scriptures, we might have hope.

Cessationists believe the Gifts of the Spirit and the Five-fold Ministry written about in the New Testament no longer apply in this generation. However, Romans 15:4 tells us that "everything" written in the past was for our instruction. It *all* has application in one way or another! Furthermore, who gets to say what passed away and what didn't? Who gets to say what gets thrown out and what still applies? That is a very dangerous way to interpret the Scriptures.

Secondly, we must also consider the experiences of modern-day Christians and compare them to what we see modeled in the Bible. Experiences that are validated in the Bible will eclipse theology void of experiences every time.

For example, when we read in the Word of God that the first-century Christians administered healing and cast out demons, and we see those same things being done by Christians around the world today, then the best-argued cessationist position seems irrational. If you tried to tell someone in a swimming pool that there's no water in the pool, he would only have to splash around to prove otherwise. What he knows to be true, plus his personal experience, is proof enough without any words even being spoken. He's proving you wrong by *showing* you. And hundreds of thousands of Christians worldwide are proving cessationists wrong by healing the sick, casting out demons, and operating in the Gifts of the Spirit.

For the intellectually honest person, the demonstration of the continuation of Spiritual Gifts is where the argument should stop. Simply observing the experiences of modern-day Christians around the world that are consistent with Biblical history should put the debate to rest. I too have seen and been used to help administer God's healing touch at times in my own ministry, as well as seen people delivered from demonic oppression and possession.

I could provide many personal examples along these lines. Here are three:

> **There are hundreds of thousands of Christians around the world today who are proving cessationists wrong by healing the sick, casting out demons, and operating in the Gifts of the Spirit.**

Many years ago, a man in our church was diagnosed with Stage 3 lung cancer, confirmed by three different medical specialists. One Sunday morning, we laid hands on him and prayed, commanding healing into his body. Upon his next visit to the oncologist, his tests came up negative. No cancer anymore! Hallelujah! He has remained healthy and whole ever since.

A lady from out of town contacted me asking for prayer. She was looking for a church that believed in and preached healing so someone could agree with her in faith. She found us online and called. I learned she had been diagnosed with thyroid cancer, and she and her husband were separated. She asked me to pray for her health and marriage. As she was talking, I felt directed by the Holy Spirit to speak with her about forgiveness and letting go of bitterness. She acknowledged she was having difficulty forgiving her husband and a few other people in her life. So, we prayed first for God to help her release these individuals in her heart of her judgments, asking the Father to forgive her unforgiveness. I then prayed for her healing and the restoration of her marriage. She called back two weeks later to tell me she was given a clean bill of health and all traces of cancer were gone, and she and her husband had reconciled! Praise God!

One Sunday, a newcomer to our church asked one of the ladies in our congregation to pray for him after the service. He had been having chronic headaches, and he knew God often used this woman to pray for the sick and see healing. But when she prayed for him, his eyes rolled back in his head, and he became agitated and slightly disoriented. She stopped praying and came to me, asking if I would take over. When I began praying, I placed my left hand on his upper back, and as I did, I felt his body become wobbly. As I continued praying, his balance gave way and he fell backward. I tried to hold him up, but his weight was too much for my one hand to catch his fall. He collapsed against the wall and slid down onto the floor. When I recognized what was happening, my prayers turned to commands. I commanded the spirit of infirmity to come out of him and return to the abyss in the name of Jesus! As I did this, the man instantly began to weep and speak in tongues, the latter of which he had never done before. Still lying on the floor, he raised his hands and began worshiping God. When I finally helped him to his feet a few moments later, his eyes and face had a different and brighter countenance. He was healed and free of demonic oppression! May God be praised!

Therefore, claiming that God no longer heals and no longer casts out demons is like telling me there's no water in the pool while I'm doing the backstroke! Furthermore, to suggest God no longer delivers people from infirmity and demonic oppression is to suggest that Jesus and the early Church cast out demons, but God has left people today to remain demonized without hope. *That is not true!* The name of Jesus is still as powerful today as it was in the first century.

I praise God for giving us the tools to deal with infirmities and the kingdom of darkness. Yet even sharing experiences like these is unconvincing to some people who cry foul based on what they claim are faked healings and deliverances. There is *some* legitimacy to that claim, as there have indeed been instances of shady people who have exploited the ministry by using manipulative techniques to line their own pockets. However, this does not nullify the anointings of ministers who conduct themselves with integrity and who operate in genuine supernatural power. While shifty imposters posing as ministers of the gospel have been around since the first century, people steeped in rigid religious customs have been around longer than that. Like the Pharisees during the days of Jesus' earthly ministry, some nullify the Word of God due to human traditions (see Mark 7:13). Therefore, since even sharing personal experiences will not convince some people bound by such traditions, let us turn our attention to the Scriptures for guidance.

We Have Not Yet Reached "Fullness" in Christ

The next problem with the claim that the Five-Fold Ministry passed away with the first century is a point covered in our master text. Let's look again at Ephesians 4:11-13.

> *[11]And it was He [God] who gave some to be apostles, some to be prophets, some to be evangelists, and some to be pastors and teachers, [12]to equip the saints for works of ministry and to build up the body of Christ, [13]until we all reach unity in the faith and in the knowledge of the Son of God, as we mature to the full measure of the stature of Christ.*

Notice these Gifts were given not only for divine revelation, but also for equipping the saints for works of the ministry, which includes evangelism, ministry to the poor, teaching proper doctrine, etc.

Next, it says these Five-Fold Ministry Gifts are necessary to build up the body of Christ *"until* we all reach *unity"* in the faith and in the knowledge of the Son of God. **This obviously hasn't**

happened yet, or else we wouldn't have factions today known as cessationists and continuationists. We also wouldn't have the 45,000 Christian denominations globally segregating themselves into their isolated groups because of their pet doctrines and methodologies. **This fact alone disproves the cessationist position because for the Five-Fold Ministry to pass away as unnecessary, the Body of Christ must reach unity *first*.**

Notice another condition for the Five-Fold Ministry to no longer be necessary: Christians must first mature to the **"full measure of the stature of Christ."** This full measure of maturity hasn't yet happened either. I don't know a single human on this planet who has reached that point, and the text says we *all* must *fully* mature in Christ before these ministry Gifts are deactivated. When will this be? When we get to heaven or when Christ returns!

The Five-Fold Ministry Gifts are essential to help grow and mature followers of Christ. When we have reached the completion of our journey and are in the arms of our Savior, having entered a realm of perfect unity and complete maturity in the full measure of the stature of Christ Himself, *then and only then* will these gifts no longer be necessary.

What then is meant by the "fullness of Christ?"

Again, when every man, woman, and child reach perfect maturity in Christ (Colossians 1:28), only then can we truly claim we, His Body, His Church, are completely filled with Him and have left the world and our sinful desires far behind. When we have totally died to self and are living in harmonious union with Him, when we are lovingly and perfectly obeying Him fully without sin or reservation, it's then when the "full measure of the stature of Christ" has come. The Five-Fold Ministry Gifts will continue to be operational and necessary as long as we live in our mortal, fallen bodies, and these Gifts will fall silent when we reach our heavenly abode.

The Five-Fold ministries are not the only Gifts mentioned in the Bible, by the way. They do represent the *primary* ministry Gifts, but the Apostle Paul mentions other Spiritual Gifts to aid the Church in reaching maturity. For example,

> *[7]Now to each one the manifestation of the Spirit is given for the common good. [8]To one there is given through the Spirit the message of wisdom, to another the message of knowledge by the same Spirit, [9]to another faith by the same Spirit, to another gifts of healing by that one Spirit, [10]to another the working of miracles, to another prophecy, to another distinguishing between spirits, to another speaking in various tongues, and to still another the interpretation of tongues. [11]All these are the work of one and the same Spirit, who apportions them to each one as He determines.* -1 Corinthians 12:7-11

Likewise, Romans 12:7-8 lists still more Gifts given to the Church such as serving, encouraging, giving (generosity), leading, and showing mercy.

Just because you don't find yourself among the Five-Fold Ministry in Ephesians 4 or possessing one of the Gifts mentioned in First Corinthians 12 or Romans 12 doesn't mean you don't have a useful gift. The Gifts listed in these passages were likely never intended to be exhaustive, because many other giftings exist that are very beneficial for the health of the Church. Some of these include singing, playing instruments well, administrative skills, craftsmanship, art and design, hospitality, writing, etc. There are several examples of these throughout the Old and New Testaments.

Likewise, there is also the Gift of *intercession*, which refers to intense and constant prayer on behalf of others, such as Anna in the Temple when Jesus was born (see Luke 2:36-38). Some people seem drawn to hours in prayer without fatiguing, while for others this is difficult.

Can you see how much the people of God need one another? This is why God sovereignly gathers people together whom He has gifted in various ways to help shore up local churches and strengthen the brethren.

It is important to point out that whenever God has invested a Gift or talent in one of His children, He expects a return on that investment. His purpose for these divine abilities is to build up the Body of Christ. As such, He wants us to offer our abilities back to Him for His use. As 1 Peter 4:10 instructs,

> **Each of you should use whatever gift you have received to serve others, as faithful stewards of God's grace in its various forms.** *(NIV)*

The Five-Fold Ministry exists to help equip the rest of the saints to do the "front line" work of God's Kingdom in the community and world. Hence, we are *all* called to minister because God wants His Church to grow, expand, and thrive. This is why Satan is constantly working to divide believers and thus weaken local churches because he knows a united Church functioning in all these Gifts is dangerous to his kingdom.

Five-Fold ministers were given to the Church by Jesus according to Ephesians 4:11. We need *every* ministry God has provided, not just two or three. These offices are *God's* idea, and there is no scriptural or historical evidence that they have died out. But one would not have to look very far to observe these gifts in operation around the world.

Regrettably, some segments of the Church have settled for pastors alone and discarded the other ministry Gifts. But pastors cannot effectively minister alone. Pastors do often have more than one Gift but rarely does a pastor possess all five. Thus, most churches are incomplete without these other Gifts, stretching pastors too thin and trying to compensate for the deficiencies.

> *Satan is constantly at work attempting to divide believers and thus weaken local churches because he knows a united church functioning in all these Gifts is dangerous to his kingdom.*

Speaking of pastors, note that cessationists apparently concede pastors are still in operation. But how can this be if the Five-Fold Ministry passed away? If the Five-Fold Ministry passed away, then this would include pastors. Yet how could the Five-Fold Ministry have passed away if pastors clearly still exist and are in operation? **It can't be both ways; it has to be one or the other.**

The Cessationist Claims against Apostles and Prophets

Cessatioinists don't seem to mind pastors, teachers, and evangelists. It's the apostles and prophets they take exception to. As already stated, if one is to be consistent regarding the claim the Five-Fold Ministry passed away, then all five need to be done away with, not just two. Why did apostles and prophets supposedly die out in the first century, but pastors, teachers, and evangelists didn't?

There is evidence in the book of Revelation suggesting the believers in Ephesus were continuationists who believed the ministry role of apostles continued to function. In Revelation 2:2(b), Jesus said, **"I know that you cannot tolerate those who are evil, and you have tested and exposed as liars those who falsely claim to be apostles."** This passage is not referring to all apostles dying out and their ministry roles ceasing to function. It means the elders in the church of Ephesus had a filtering system to process those who had claims of being apostles. Their purpose was to examine *incoming* apostles. They didn't say, "No one else can be an apostle." They just had systems in place to test those who made that claim to verify if their claims were authentic, just as we should be doing today with those who claim to have a pastoral gift. The Ephesians believed the work of the Five-Fold Ministry was continuing after the first apostles!

Concerning prophets, cessationists claim God isn't speaking through anyone anymore since the Bible has been completed. However, please note **the Word of God never says anywhere that the Bible is the only way God speaks.** If this were the case, we wouldn't have pastors, and none of us could ever hope to hear the voice of God on our own! The Bible says those who belong to Him know His voice!

> *My sheep hear My voice; I know them, and they follow Me.* -John 10:27

> *For as many as are led by the Spirit of God are sons of God.* -Romans 8:14

Even cessationists believe God "speaks" to them and leads them in certain aspects of their lives. And this leading would be considered extra-Biblical since there would be no chapter and verse in the Bible saying, "Mr. So-and-So, marry Suzy, and the two of you go to Africa as missionaries and spread the Word of God there." Yet many cessationists do precisely that sort of thing because they feel "led" to do so. But where is this specific guidance provided in the Bible? It's not there. Wouldn't this be operating as one's own prophet, according to the cessationist view? Wouldn't this be "adding to Scripture"? If God isn't speaking anymore because the Bible is completed, no one would ever sense this sort of leading and guidance of the Holy Spirit. Yet cessationists would be some of the first people to say they have indeed sensed specific types of leadings from God, which violates their theology.

Similarly, cessationists will often say, "I'll pray about it," in reference to asking God for guidance in situations not explicitly addressed in Scripture where they need the leading of the Holy Spirit. For example, a pastor may approach a woman and ask her to serve in the children's ministry. Reluctant to answer immediately, she responds, "I'll pray about it and get back to you, Pastor." Praying for direction assumes God is going to speak in some way through an inner knowing or another method of guidance. Yet somehow, cessationists nevertheless claim God is no longer speaking. Again, it can't be both ways.

How does this sort of theology make Christianity any different from pagan religions, where people speak to a god, but their god never speaks back in any form? On the contrary, the God of all creation *does* speak in ways which are extra-Biblical. God never speaks anything *anti-Biblical* because He will never violate His Word. But the Holy Spirit does provide additional guidance on matters the Word of God does not specifically address. Isn't that wonderful?

3

THE GIFTS OF THE SPIRIT

Gifts of the Spirit refer to a list of divine abilities for the further enrichment of the Church. On this subject, the Apostle Paul wrote to the Corinthian church, stating, **"Now concerning spiritual gifts, brethren, I do not want you to be ignorant"** (1 Corinthians 12:1). And then the great Apostle elaborated on those Gifts, which include special wisdom (v. 8), and the message of knowledge (v. 8), or what some might call a "word of knowledge," which is the special ability to know information about someone or something which could only be revealed by the Spirit of God.

Listed also is the Gift of faith (v. 9), which would pertain to a special kind of faith over and above faith for salvation. This kind of faith usually expresses itself in the Gift of healing (v. 9) and other various miracles (v. 10). Verse 10 goes on to list prophecy (the ability to predict the future by the Spirit of God), the discerning of spirits (a supernatural ability to discern if something is from the spirit of God or not), tongues (the ability to speak in unlearned languages), and interpretation of tongues.

Toward the end of that chapter, Paul also listed Gifts of administration and assistance (v. 28). There are people in every church who are not called to the platform, and don't want to be. They find their fulfilment and call from God assisting with matters of money administration and helping with other behind-the-scenes details of helping the ministry run smoothly.

Paul once again also mentions the role of apostles, prophets, and teachers. Paul says in this discourse that all these Gifts are the working of the same Spirit, and He distributes them among the members of the Church as He sees fit (v. 11).

On the matter of tongues, this topic appears in numerous places in the New Testament. As already mentioned, the Gift of tongues is the divine ability to speak in languages not learned. It is often a language of the world (see Acts 2:1-12), and sometimes it is a dialect of heaven (see 1 Corinthians 14:2). It was a Gift of God given to the early Church as a sign and a spiritual tool in prayer. I will elaborate on tongues in the epilogue at the end of the book.

The issue we want to grapple with here is whether these various Gifts passed away in the first century.

> *To attempt to pasteurize and homogenize God and His Word into what our puny human minds can comfortably accept is tantamount to idolatry.*

I will begin this part of our discussion by saying I realize the Gifts of the Spirit, and particularly speaking in tongues, are regarded as bizarre by the uninitiated. But allow me to point out that simply going to church and reading out of an ancient book is seen as equally peculiar and lacking intelligence by millions of other people who have no time for God, church, or the Bible. *Pick your poison.* **If you are in Christ, one way or another someone is going to find you odd, bigoted, and even utterly out of touch with reality.**

God did not ask our permission to satisfy our feeble intellects to do what He does. His ways are not our ways, and His thoughts are not our thoughts (see Isaiah 55:8). In fact, **God will often** *violate our intellects on purpose* for at least two reasons: First, to demonstrate that He is God, and we are not, and secondly, to show us the need to walk by faith and not by sight (2 Corinthians 5:7). Therefore, to attempt to pasteurize and homogenize God and His Word into what our puny human minds can comfortably accept is tantamount to idolatry. I had to figure this out the hard way.

I was raised in the more charismatic and Pentecostal streams of Christianity, and I saw numerous cases of abuse of the Spiritual Gifts, including behaviors I regarded as freakish. After spending several years in a church in my late twenties and early thirties that believed in and taught about the Gifts of the Spirit, I eventually catapulted in the other direction, wishing not to associate myself with practices I could not explain to my intellectual satisfaction. My family and I settled in for a time at a church where I knew I would never have to see anything that disturbed my intellect. During this time, I set out to write a book refuting the practice of speaking in tongues. However, I abandoned that work after several weeks because my research kept validating the modern-day practice of tongues rather than refuting it. I finally threw up my hands and exclaimed, "Ok, Lord. If Your Word says it, and I can't refute it, then I'm forced to agree." It was at that point I became more receptive to the Gifts of the Spirit and went on to operate in them myself, which I will talk more about in the epilogue.

Let us endeavor to avoid both extremes on the spiritual spectrum. The first extreme would be interpreting the Word of God *solely* through the lens of personal experience, and the second is giving no room for the outflow of experience as we live out our faith. In endeavoring to avoid these unbiblical extremes, we will now move on to assess the cessationist reasoning on the matter of Gifts of the Spirit and consider it against a close examination of Scripture.

The Pillar of the Cessationist Movement

The passage of choice used in attempting to support cessationist theology regarding Gifts of the Spirit is First Corinthians 13:8-10.

> ⁸*Love never fails. But where there are prophecies, they will cease; where there are tongues, they will be restrained; where there is knowledge, it will be dismissed. ⁹For we know in part and we prophesy in part, ¹⁰but when the perfect comes, the partial passes away.*

This passage tells us that Gifts of the Spirit would at some point become obsolete after the writing of First Corinthians. But when will this be? According to cessationists, it was at the completion of the canon of Scripture. However, there are several problems with this interpretation.

First, we know knowledge still exists. If we interpret this passage according to the cessationist view, then we have to throw out knowledge along with tongues and prophecy. Once again, you can't have it both ways. If tongues and prophecy ceased to exist when Scripture was completed, so did knowledge. And if knowledge still exists, so do the other two. You can't cherry-pick the one you like and throw out the others. Accurate Bible interpretation doesn't work that way.

What kind of knowledge are we talking about then? Is it simply general knowledge, or "words of knowledge," as in the seer anointing? Or both?

The Greek term for knowledge used here is *gnosis*, which means a *knowing, knowledge, wisdom, doctrine*. The literal meaning refers to proper doctrine, wisdom, and head knowledge. In the context of this passage, however, we could make the case that it's talking about "words of knowledge," such as the seer anointing, but it doesn't specifically say. It simply says *gnosis*, the same word for understanding or head knowledge used elsewhere in Scripture, such as Luke 1:77: *"...to give His people knowledge [gnosis] of salvation."* Thus, we could conclude that the knowledge Paul is talking about in First Corinthians doesn't specifically refer to the seer anointing, but to general knowledge, wisdom, understanding in the human mind, and dissemination of proper doctrine. This kind of knowledge still exists, obviously, or you wouldn't be reading this book right now.

To further bolster this point, what were the first-century apostles using as their basis for preaching and teaching proper doctrine? Operating in the seer anointing with "words of knowledge" was certainly a part of this process, but notice the Bible says when the first-century apostles preached and taught doctrine, they did it using the Old Testament Scriptures as the backdrop. So yes, the Old Testament has always pointed to Christ, and the teachers in the first-century Church used them persuasively to teach proper doctrine.

> *For he [Apollos] powerfully refuted the Jews in public debate, showing by the Scriptures [Old Testament] that Jesus was the Christ.* -Acts 18:28

Remember, at this point in history the New Testament wasn't yet written. Instead, Apollos used the Old Testament to preach proper doctrine about Christ. There are other references to Paul, Peter, Philip, and Stephen all basing their preaching on the Old Testament. What were they doing? They weren't using "words of knowledge," but rather disseminating knowledge from the Old Testament Scriptures because this was all they had at the time. But this was sufficient since the Old Testament points to Christ.

The point is that the "knowledge" mentioned in First Corinthians 13:8-10 doesn't specifically refer *only* to the divine Gift of Word of Knowledge. Again, the Greek word for knowledge used there is *gnosis*, which denotes wisdom, doctrine, and knowledge in general. This sort of knowledge is still disseminated today. If we throw out tongues and prophecy as having passed away, then we must reject the dissemination of knowledge along with it. And no logical person would say the dissemination of knowledge has passed away.

The Bible is not a smorgasbord of ideas where you can pick out what you like and reject the rest. You must receive it *all* as the revelation from God that it is.

When Will the Gifts to the Church Pass Away?

When will prophecy, tongues, and knowledge as we know them cease? The apostle Paul answers in the same text: **"When the perfect comes"** (First Corinthians 13:10). The Greek word translated into "perfect" is *teleios*, which *means perfection, having reached its end, completeness,* and according to Strong's Concordance refers specifically to the **"completeness of Christian character."** This is extremely important to our discussion because cessationists believe this passage refers to the completed Scripture canon. However, this cannot be the case for two reasons.

First, the word *teleios* is referring explicitly to the completeness of Christian character, which will not happen until we are in the presence of Christ in Heaven. Secondly, verse 12 goes on to say,

> **"For now we see through a glass, darkly; but then face to face: now I know in part; but then shall I know even as also I am known."** *(KJV)*

The Berean Literal Bible version puts it even more clearly.

> *For presently we see through a glass in obscurity;*
> *but then, face to face. Presently, I know in part;*
> *but then I will know fully, even as I have been fully*
> *known. (BLB)*

This can hardly refer to the completion of the New Testament canon for two reasons. First, we don't see Him face-to-face yet. Secondly, we who live in the body here on earth are still seeing and understanding with partial understanding as if looking through a darkened glass in "obscurity," even though we now have a completed Bible. We must have the revelation of the Spirit even to understand the Bible or have it penetrate our hardened hearts. This is why we still need the Gifts of the Spirit to help bring the revelation of the Word of God to our sinful hearts. But "then" – when we are in God's glorious presence – we will see "face to face" and will "know fully."

Paul's point is that tongues, prophecy, and the dissemination of knowledge as we know it will be unnecessary when we enter our eternal abode. For now, since we have not reached the point of perfection, God has given us Spiritual Gifts to help us grow and mature.

Hence, the cessationist view of Gifts of the Spirit being operative only during the first century to provide special revelation until the completion of the New Testament is shown to be incorrect based on the very passage they use to try to prove their position.

Sometimes cessationists will point out that the words used for the cessation of *knowledge* and *prophecy* in First Corinthians 13 are in the passive tense in the original Greek text, indicating an outside force will halt them. However, the verb used for the cessation of *tongues* is in the middle tense, which may indicate that tongues will cease on their own. This is regarded by cessationists as further evidence that tongues were temporary and would simply expire when the need was no longer there. But this sort of grammatical analysis leaves out a critical observation from the Greek.

You see, at the risk of getting too deep into the interpretation of the ancient languages, let's just quickly consider that some verbs typically take the *middle tense*. The Greek verb, *pauó*, translated in First Corinthians 13:8 as "be stilled" by the New International Version and "vanish" in the King James is one of them. Even so, there is no particular significance to the change from passive to middle tense in this passage referring to tongues when we consider the context and its use in other places in Scripture. In Luke 8:24, for example, when Jesus and His disciples were in a boat caught in severe weather, it says the storm was "stilled" (*pauó*), the same word and tense used in First Corinthians 13:8 to describe tongues. In this case, Jesus *actively* stilled the storm; it didn't settle down on its own. Thus, the argument regarding the middle or passive tense is extraneous. It's irrelevant, and it doesn't hold up.

Cessationists argue that if tongues, prophecy, and knowledge continue, this continuation of the use of the Gifts would in effect be adding to Scripture, which the Bible forcefully warns against (see Revelation 22:18). However, most continuationists do not consider these Gifts and divine impartations as taking the place of Scripture or adding to it, but more like the "leading of the Spirit" in situations not clearly addressed in the Bible.

Many cessationists feel the same way regarding God's leading in their own lives. As already pointed out, I'll reiterate that cessationists commonly claim God led or "told" them to do something.

"God told me to take this particular job."

"God led me to that particular church."

"God led me to the mission field."

They would maintain these are instances of guidance or communication from God but would never place it on par with the Bible. And this is the same way continuationists see the Gifts of the Spirit providing guidance from the Holy Spirit on matters the Word of God does not specifically address.

Hence, the state of "perfection" or "completeness" First Corinthians 13:8-12 speaks of is our eternal home in Heaven. At that time, there will be no more need for miraculous Gifts such as tongues and prophecy because we will know everything fully and be complete in Christ.

The continuationist view does not rule out the possibility that the need for the more supernatural gifts might fluctuate according to the need of the moment or even an individual's faith. But there is absolutely nothing in the text in First Corinthians 13 suggesting these Gifts will stop when the canon of Scripture is complete. If there are any compelling historical and theological arguments for the cessationist position on Gifts of the Spirit, it certainly isn't supported in First Corinthians 13.

4

WHAT DO WE MAKE OF
PERSONAL EXPERIENCE?

Revival in the Last Days

At the time of this writing, a revival has suddenly broken out among the students at the small Asbury University in Wilmore, Kentucky. Asbury is a Christian college affiliated with the Methodists, a very conservative denomination in their theology and practice. They are not known for outward displays of passionate worship or the exercise of Gifts of the Spirit. Methodists tend to be very restrained in their religious expression, leaning more toward tradition and ritual to some extent. Yet the chapel meetings at Asbury transformed into worship services that look more like Pentecostal or charismatic gatherings. People have flooded the altar area at the front of the room, bowing down in reverence, raising their hands in adoration of Jesus, crying out in hunger for God, and worshiping Him with uncommon fervor. Reports are emerging of people baptized in the Holy Spirit with the evidence of speaking in tongues, as well as an instance of at least one person who manifested demonic oppression and was delivered with the help of a bystander who was experienced in deliverance ministry. The Asbury revival has so transformed the campus that the chapel services are ongoing 24 hours per day, seven days per week. The presence of God is reported to be so tangible that people have flooded the chapel services from every State and various foreign countries to experience a unique touch from God. And now, the revival has spread to dozens of other university campuses and churches nationwide and abroad.

God is up to something unusual in these last days, and this move of His Spirit is marked by experiences not common to the sleepy Sunday morning rituals of many Americanized church services today. This revival is resulting in a new hunger and fervor for the deeper things of God, and by His sovereign hand this new spiritual awakening is happening among young people! Praise God!

In walking with Christ for three decades, I have learned by experience that God rejects confinement to our narrow theological ideas of Him. Instead, He will often break out of our doctrinal boxes and express Himself in ways that are surprising, even shocking at times. Jesus rocked the religious world of Jewish culture by doing and saying things that put people back on their heels. Jesus once even spit on the ground and made a paste with the mud and spittle that He smeared on a blind man's eyes to heal him! The hallmark of revival is this same tendency of God to disrupt the norm during certain times throughout history, bringing people to a place of desperation for Him that ritual and doctrine alone cannot satisfy.

How to Properly Evaluate Experience

At this point in the discussion, I wish to make a clarifying statement. At no time do I wish to elevate experience over the Word of God. There have unfortunately been some who have done this to their harm. I agree with the words of John R.W. Stott in his 1974 book, *Baptism and Fullness:*

> "Only when the word of God dwells in us richly shall we be able to evaluate the experiences which we and others may have. Experience must never be the criterion for truth; truth must always be the criterion for experience."

Likewise, at no time do I wish to advance a strictly academic treatment of the Scriptures to the point of dismissing the significance of encounters. If the Bible is anything, it is a chronicling of people who had encounters with God, and they are written down for our guidance and admonition. John R.W. Stott also wrote in the same book,

> "[Some] lay such emphasis on the sufficiency of Christ that they seem to have a static concept of the Christian life which allows no room either for growth into maturity or for deeper, fuller experiences of Christ."

There's no question that God uses experiences with His presence to bring blessings to countless people. After such encounters, many Christians have testified to having experienced new liberty, release from inner bondages and inhibitions, freedom from addictions, an overflow of joy and peace, a stronger sense of the presence of God, a deeper sense of love toward people, and a new zeal and boldness in evangelism. These encounters with the Holy Spirit of God should raise our expectations, thus challenging all mediocre Christian living and stodgy, supercilious church life.

It behooves us to recall that some of the notable leaders of Church history still revered today had their own spiritual experiences. Dwight L. Moody and Charles Finney each recorded such experiences. As we read their accounts of profound spiritual and emotional encounters with the Holy Spirit of God, we are unwise to dismiss them as the fanatical ravings of emotionalized fellows who lack intelligence. These were brilliant leaders. Yet Finney wrote in his journal that his inexplicable encounter with the Holy Spirit caused him to bellow with "unutterable gushings of my heart."

Other examples of the supernatural touching the ordinary abound. For instance, I have known two men who were *instantly* delivered from extreme cigarette addiction through such divine encounters. I also once saw a visitor to our church shuffle in with a walker and leave carrying it out!

In chapter two, I provided some testimonies regarding healings and deliverances in my ministry. These testimonies are similar to the reports of healings and deliverances we see in the New Testament, both in Jesus' ministry and the book of Acts. These experiences are relevant as we attempt to understand Spiritual Gifts and their application in today's Church culture.

Martin Lloyd Jones once said, "The gospel was authenticated in signs and wonders. The Scriptures never say anywhere that these things were only temporary – *never!* There is no such statement anywhere."

The cessationist view fails to acknowledge this. And it also fails to recognize the tens of millions of Christians around the world who claim to operate in the Gifts of the Spirit, particularly speaking in tongues. Are all of them lying or faking it? Such a notion wouldn't even be intellectually honest. In a court of law, when the experience or testimony of even a few people who don't know each other line up, this is usually considered solid admissible evidence. But we aren't talking about a handful of people who don't know each other. We're talking about *tens of millions of them*, not only in this era but for the last 2,000 years. Nearly every major revival around the world since the time of Christ was marked with supernatural experiences, including speaking in tongues.

As one example, the famous Azusa Street revival, which lasted nine years from 1906 to 1915 in Los Angeles, was best known for its outpouring of supernatural experiences, which included but were not limited to speaking in tongues and dramatic miracles of healing. These same manifestations have been experienced by countless people all over the world since the time of Christ up to the present.

> *Martin Lloyd Jones once said, "The gospel was authenticated in signs and wonders. The Scriptures never say anywhere that these things were only temporary – never! There is no such statement anywhere."*

So, are all of us who speak in tongues insane? Are all who have experienced a miracle delusional? Or might there be something beyond the intellect for which cessationist theology makes no room?

No Second-Rate Christians

It's important to point out that *not* speaking in tongues or operating in the other Gifts of the Spirit doesn't make a person less loved by God. It has been my experience that some cessationists may have embraced this view because having been made to feel as though they were second-rate Christians. In some cases, someone may have made them feel as though they were castaways for not having been endowed with any of the Spiritual Gifts.

I once had a conversation with such a man. He had been taking me to task for my views on the Five-Fold Ministry, so I asked him to give me a chapter and verse of a place in the Bible proving the Five-Fold Ministry passed away. And, of course, he could offer no such Biblical reference. But he kept repeating, "Not having any of these Gifts doesn't make me less of a Christian." And I kept reiterating that I never said it did. This argument was the only one he could lean on, however, because he had no Biblical support for his beliefs. It became clear to me this was more of an emotional issue with him because someone had likely offended him, or he was made to feel like a lesser Christian in some way.

Allow me to say how sorry I am if you are one of those who was treated in a hurtful way. But sometimes, it's not even how people are treated that makes them feel like castaways. Instead, it's the feeling that comes over them as they hear someone talk about Spiritual Gifts or observes someone who operates in them. For example, seeing someone minister deliverance to a suffering person or hearing a person talk about the exciting new elements of their faith that tongues or prophecy have opened to them might cause someone who has never experienced these things to feel a bit insecure. But it shouldn't.

You see, God gives His people Gifts for the enrichment of those who *seek* them. They are available to those who **"eagerly desire the greater gifts"** (see 1 Corinthians 12:31). The word translated into "desire" in this verse is the Greek word *zéloó*, which means *to desire jealously*. The Cognate Word Study says the word implies *"to be deeply committed to something, with the implication of accompanying desire – to be earnest, to set one's heart on, to be completely intent upon."* These Gifts are available to all God's children, but we must seek them with earnest desire.

Some have said that Paul's admonition to "eagerly desire the greater gifts" was referring to love. The context, however, suggests otherwise. Paul's exhortation was on the heels of elucidating Spiritual Gifts. He was saying that while not everyone will operate in all the Gifts he listed, we should nevertheless desire to operate in at least some of them. And that was a springboard for him to switch gears and talk about the *motive* we should have for using the Spiritual Gifts, which is the motive of love.

If a person chooses not to participate in the Spiritual Gifts, that is his or her prerogative. Or if, for some reason, someone doesn't experience any of these divine Gifts, it doesn't mean he or she isn't saved. On the contrary, such a person will still make it to Heaven if he or she clings to Christ as Savior.

There are many reasons why someone may not operate in the Gifts of the Spirit. One reason is because of being repelled by the strange behavior of people who claim to operate in these Gifts. I understand and sympathize. I, too, have been befuddled by the behavior I have observed in some church services. But we mustn't throw the baby out with the bathwater.

While I have been offended and disgusted in the past by the anti-biblical methods of people on both ends of the spectrum, charismatics and ultra-conservatives alike, I nevertheless find myself continually drawn back to the things of the Spirit despite a few oddities I have witnessed. I could probably write another entire book on the manipulative methods and the kooky concepts to which some Christians and ministers adhere. I have been the victim of what I'll call *spiritual abuse* by certain ministers who cared more about their reputations than the spiritual well-being of those to whom they ministered. If I were judging the legitimacy of Spiritual Gifts based solely on my experiences with those who misused them, I would certainly run in the other direction. The Holy Spirit, however, has been gracious to me by helping me put my feelings aside and recognize practices that are biblical compared to ones that are not. And knowing God's Word on these matters also helps, of course!

I identify very well with the late Pastor Jack Hayford in his book *A Passion for Fullness* when writing about his own encounters with excess.

> "Even though I have often been disturbed by excesses and fanaticism among those who exercise

such Gifts, I have stayed in the community because I found that for every instance of excess there are a hundred examples of depth, reality and divine power."

I relate very well with people who have scorned Spiritual Gifts due to peculiar or inexplicable behavior because I used to be one of those people. Yet a hunger for deeper encounters with God, such as we see in the Scriptures, has continually drawn me back to being more open to things I cannot explain to my intellectual satisfaction. I have simply learned to "eat the meat and spit out the bones," as the saying goes.

Another reason people may not operate in the Spiritual Gifts may be a lack of teaching on them and thus ignorance about their significance, or simply an over-analysis of how they will come rather than just flowing in faith.

We must also remember that 1 Corinthians 12:11 says the Spirit of God distributes these gifts as *He* determines. This raises a question as to whether the Gift of tongues is available to everyone or only to those whom God chooses. In First Corinthians 12:30, Paul asks, "Do all have gifts of healing? Do all speak in tongues? Do all interpret?"

In the context of that section, he asks the question for emphasis because the obvious answer is no, not everyone has been gifted in this way. However, Paul wrote in the same letter in chapter 14 verse 5 that he wished *all* would speak in tongues and prophesy. We must not diminish the significance of Paul's statement. He believed speaking in tongues was so important that he wished all of God's people would do it!

Furthermore, we see in the book of Acts that whenever the Holy Spirit came upon a person after salvation, this experience was always accompanied by speaking in tongues without exception. One such example is found in Acts 19.

¹While Apollos was at Corinth, Paul passed through the interior and came to Ephesus. There he found some disciples ²and asked them, "Did you receive the Holy Spirit when you became believers?"

"No," they answered, "we have not even heard that there is a Holy Spirit."

³"Into what, then, were you baptized?" Paul asked.

"The baptism of John," they replied.

⁴Paul explained: "John's baptism was a baptism of repentance. He told the people to believe in the One coming after him, that is, in Jesus."

⁵On hearing this, they were baptized into the name of the Lord Jesus. ⁶And when Paul laid his hands on them, the Holy Spirit came upon them, and they spoke in tongues and prophesied.

We must consider these instances of believers immediately being baptized in the Holy Spirit with the evidence of speaking in tongues if we are to understand the Gift of tongues properly.

In taking these instances into account, therefore, there appear to be different types and applications of tongues. In First Corinthians 12:10, Paul writes that there are "various tongues," implying perhaps that there are different versions of this Gift for specific functions. There appear to be certain kinds of tongues endowed only on certain people, such as the *public* use of tongues and interpretation of tongues to bring a special revelation from the Holy Spirit. Not everyone is going to function in this Gift, apparently, at least not on a regular basis.

However, the *private* use of praying in tongues appears to be available to everyone, as indicated throughout the book of Acts and 1 Corinthians 14:4, the latter of which tells us that anyone who speaks in tongues "edifies himself." This is probably why the Apostle Paul wanted everyone to speak in tongues, because it is a method for building oneself up spiritually.

Therefore, I suggest educating yourself further on the Spiritual Gifts, especially if you would like to receive one or more but do not know how. (See the resource list at the end of this book.) It comes down to earnestly desiring them, asking God, and receiving by faith. Often, they come about with the aid of the laying of hands and prayer by an anointed man or woman of God. (I elaborate on this further in the epilogue.)

I say again that not experiencing these Gifts doesn't make a person a second-rate Christian. Of equal importance, claiming something isn't valid just because it hasn't been personally experienced is not only dismissive to those who *have* experienced it, but also intellectually dishonest. In this case, it also lacks scriptural and historical support.

> *Claiming something isn't valid just because it hasn't been personally experienced is not only dismissive to those who have experienced it, but also intellectually dishonest. In this case, it also lacks scriptural and historical support.*

Rather than judging one another based on exercising these Gifts or *not* exercising them, perhaps a better and more godly approach would be to learn to love and cheer one another on as we grow together. We should also learn to appreciate another's Gifts and abilities because each one was given for the enrichment of the entire Body of Christ. We cannot grow to maturity without one another.

As it says in First Corinthians 12,

> ¹²**The body is a unit, though it is composed of many parts. And although its parts are many, they all form one body. So it is with Christ. ²⁰As it is, there are many parts, but one body.**

It's Important How We Regard the Supernatural

In the days Jesus walked the earth, there were factions among the teachers of the law. There was a religious sect known as the Sadducees, the Jewish aristocrats of their day. They believed the Torah (the first five books of the Old Testament) was the only authority on matters of life and faith. They flatly refused oral tradition or any writing that would come after the Torah, such as the book of Proverbs, Psalms, Isaiah, etc. They believed all divine revelation stopped with the Torah. *They were history's first cessationists!* As such, the Sadducees rejected entirely the supernatural.

The group known as the Pharisees were united with the Sadducees in their opposition to Jesus but divided in their views on the supernatural. Acts 23:8 says the Pharisees believed in spirits, angels, and the resurrection of the dead, while the Sadducees denied the existence of all of them. Yet both groups believed in Jehovah and studied the same scrolls of the Torah.

There is nothing new under the sun. The faction we have today with cessationists and continuationists is reminiscent of the Sadducees and Pharisees. We must be very careful, for if we deny the continuation of God's supernatural work in the present, we are siding with the same seducing spirit that deceived the Sadducees.

Jesus once said to the Sadducees in Matthew 22:29, **"You are mistaken because you do not know the Scriptures or the power of God."** Such a rebuke must have been a terrible barb to the egos of the Sadducees since they prided themselves in mastering the Scriptures. Yet Jesus said, "You don't know the Scriptures nor the power of God." In other words, they had eyes but could not see and ears but could not hear. They studied God's Word, but their understanding was darkened on its deeper meanings like so many people today. In their intellectual pride, they became puffed up with the pomp of their strictly academic treatment of God's holy Word, just like so many people today, and in doing so extinguish the Spirit.

First Thessalonians 5:20 is our guide here: **Do not extinguish the Spirit. Do not treat prophecies with contempt...**

Second Timothy 3:5 also tells us that in the last days, there would be people who would have a **"form of godliness but deny its power."** It goes on to say to *avoid such people!* They are like the Sadducees of Jesus' day. They have some intellectual understanding of the Bible, yet they do not discern with spiritual eyes when they read it. We must be people who wish to be *changed* by the Word, not change the Word to fit our comforts. The latter would be playing right into Satan's devices.

It is an implausible argument that Satan would plot to infiltrate the Church with a strategy to get people to operate in the Gifts of the Spirit and pursue the Five-Fold Ministry. He would be fighting against himself since these Gifts strengthen the Church and God's people. Jesus said a house divided against itself will fall (see Luke 11:17). It's more likely Satan would design a tactic to entice people to believe Spiritual Gifts and the Five-Fold Ministry have passed away so he can weaken the Church and make it less effect against his dark kingdom. Remember, Satan is a liar and deceiver!

What spirit, then, are we fellowshipping with when we choose our side of this debate?

To be bluntly honest, let's just call a spade a spade. Cessationism is not represented in the Bible, which makes it a false doctrine (heresy). Therefore, I implore any cessationists who may be reading this to *"come out from among them and be separate, says the LORD"* (2 Corinthians 6:17). If you are wrong, wouldn't you want to know?

The bottom line is that Jesus Himself addressed Spiritual Gifts in the Great Commission as recorded in Mark 16:15, and these instructions have never been revoked or even slightly modified.

> *It is an implausible argument that Satan would plot to infiltrate the Church with a strategy to get people to operate in the Gifts of the Spirit and pursue the five-fold ministry. He would be fighting against himself since these Gifts strengthen the Church and God's people.*

> *[15]And He said to them, "Go into all the world and preach the gospel to every creature. [16]Whoever believes and is baptized will be saved, but whoever does not believe will be condemned. [17]And these signs will accompany those who believe: In My name they will drive out demons; they will speak in new tongues; [18]they will pick up snakes with their hands, and if they drink any deadly poison, it will not harm them; they will lay their hands on the sick, and they will be made well."*

If preaching the gospel hasn't passed away, then Spiritual Gifts remain as well because Jesus connected the signs to the preaching for those who believe. Brethren, these are the words of our Master, Jesus! Our Savior did *not* say, "These signs will follow my first apostles but will pass away when you all die out." No! He said, "These signs shall follow those who *believe!*" Period! That includes *all* followers of Christ for *all time!*

Many people don't walk in these signs with more regularity because they don't desire them. Or they may *experiment* with the Gifts, and if they don't see immediate results, they write them off and never try again. But consider again a crucial qualifier in Jesus' Great Commission. He said these signs shall follow those who "*believe.*" If a person doesn't have faith regarding this promise, then no signs shall follow.

It amazes me how we tend to cherry-pick the Bible. Cessationists don't have a problem with verses 15 and 16 of Mark chapter 16, which tell us to go into all the world and preach the gospel to every creature. Yet they *do* have a problem with the rest of Jesus' Great Commission in verses 17 and 18 regarding driving out demons, speaking with new tongues, healing the sick, etc. How can the commission to go into all the world and preach the gospel be relevant for today if the rest of the commission isn't? That doesn't make sense.

Doctrines like cessationism exist to attempt to dismiss people's disobedience and lack of success in doing the things Jesus told us to do. Allow me to therefore provide some guidance here. If you have stepped out on faith and attempted to operate in the supernatural by laying hands on people for healing and failed, what did you do next? Did you stop trying? Jesus' disciples failed on many occasions to walk in the supernatural even while they walked with the Lord. But later on the disciples finally got it right. They kept trying. They didn't give up. And incidentally, the event that catapulted their results was the Baptism of the Holy Spirit on the Day of Pentecost.

I haven't been successful with every person I have prayed for, either. Yet I *have* seen many healings and deliverances. Most of those healings and deliverances would have never taken place had I given up early on. As you and I continue to press in to carry out the Great Commission – *all of it* – I expect we will see more and more results in the days ahead. So keep trying! These signs shall follow those who believe!

I close this chapter by claiming no superior wisdom or accomplishment when it comes to Spiritual Gifts or operating in the miraculous. In fact, I feel I am woefully inexperienced compared to others who have a better track record than my own. As I have heard Andrew Wommack often say, "I haven't arrived, but at least I've left!" In other words, I'm not yet where I want to be, but I'm moving in the right direction. I identify so well with the response of the blind man when interrogated by the Pharisees in John 9:25 after Jesus healed him. ***"There is one thing I do know: I was blind, but now I see!"*** I don't have all the answers, but I know what I have seen and experienced, and those experiences are consistent with the Word of God.

5

THE FASTEST GROWING DEMOGRAPHIC IN CHRISTIANITY

It may come as a surprise that continuationists are significantly outpacing every other segment of Christianity in terms of growth. James Rutz elucidated this phenomenon in his 2005 book *Mega Shift*. Rutz did not refer to this demographic as continuationists, but rather "Core Apostolics," as this group comprises the core of the growth of Christianity worldwide.

A Core Apostolic, in Rutz' definition, refers to those who are "apostolic" in the sense that they are missionary-minded and eager to start new fellowships. Rutz also defined this group as Christ followers who believe that what began with the first apostles is continuing today, and they are, in fact, experiencing miraculous demonstrations of God's power regularly. More familiar terms for these groups would be *charismatics* and *Pentecostals*.

According to Rutz's research and numbers provided in part by Dr. Todd Johnson of *World Christian Trends*, from 1970 to 2000, charismatics and Pentecostals grew worldwide at a blistering rate of 8.8% annually, while mainstream Evangelicals limped along at a near-stagnant 1.1%. He defined these two categories as follows:

"I've placed the entire Church on a continuum. On the left side, you have the denominational folks. On the *far* left end, you have a vast pile of tradition-bound…highly centralized, and strategically useless organizations that haven't grown much since the 1940's. On the right side, you have the independents, composed of overlapping groups of known by such labels as post-denominational, neo-apostolic, radical, restorations, free, etc… [They include] independent networks which are a mix of charismatics, Pentecostals, and even [some] Evangelicals. There were just 26 million of them in 1970, but 260 million in 2000. A ten-fold increase! Added together, these two blocs are the *Core Apostolics*. From 1970 to 2000, they grew 8% a year, from 71 million to 707 million."

Rutz went on to compare this growth to other world religions and found it eclipsed every other religious group. Core Apostolics were by far the fastest growing religious group on earth from 1970 to 2000, outpacing growth of Islam nearly 5 to 1. Rutz showed that Islam was growing at a pace of just under 2%, about the same as Protestants, Catholics, and nominal Christians. If Core Apostolics were removed from the equation, Christianity and Islam would show nearly identical growth rates during that time period. Thus, the dominant growth of Christianity globally during that 30-year period was fueled primarily by Core Apostolics.

But that was then, and this is now. What about *current* growth rates? According to numbers compiled by Wikipedia and reported in 2023, Pentecostalism is still the fastest growing religious movement globally. They state,

"According to various scholars and sources, **Pentecostalism** is the fastest-growing religious movement in the world; this growth is primarily due to religious conversion to Pentecostal and Charismatic Christianity. According to Pulitzer Center, 35,000 people become Pentecostal every day."

Wow!

Shouldn't we be excited about this growth? Regardless of your denominational affiliation, shouldn't we be rejoicing that Christianity is outpacing every other religion on earth, with Pentecostals leading the way?

What do we make of this trend? Why are Core Apostolics (i.e. continuationists, Pentecostals, etc.) accounting for the most significant growth worldwide than all other religious groups? It's because the power of God is being unleashed globally, and people are experiencing what cessationists erroneously say has passed away. While some Christians sit in ivory towers pontificating over theology and doctrinal dogmas, other groups are out getting their hands dirty by *doing* the work of the Kingdom and experiencing God's miraculous power as they do.

On that note, James Rutz uses the first 40 pages of his book to chronicle the jaw-dropping documented and verified miracles happening around the world among these Core Apostolics.

As one example, two Korean women went to pray for the people in a village in Uzbekistan, a Country in central Asia, in June 1999. Although they spoke only Korean, they were invited by gesture to enter a home and pray for an elderly man who was paralyzed. One of the ladies, Kim, said later, "The lame man began to wriggle and then stood up as though someone had just cut his chains. He was healed!" As the man stood to his feet, the two Korean women suddenly realized that the awed bystanders had no idea *why* he was healed. Not knowing what else to do, in desperation, Kim began explaining the gospel in Korean, hoping they would understand a few words and get the general idea. To their amazement, the people all listened in rapt attention for 20 minutes because they were all hearing her in their own language! As a result, more than 40 people became followers of Christ that day.

Does this account sound familiar? Doesn't this mirror something we've read in the Scriptures?

> *⁴And they were all filled with the Holy Spirit and began to speak in other tongues as the Spirit enabled them. ⁵Now there were dwelling in Jerusalem God-fearing Jews from every nation under heaven. ⁶And when this sound rang out, a crowd came together in bewilderment, because each one heard them speaking his own language. ⁷Astounded and amazed, they asked, "Are not all these men who are speaking Galileans? ⁸How is it then that each of us hears them in his own native language?* -Acts 2:4-8

Another instance Rutz shares happened in 2001 when a five-year-old boy named Arjun Janki Dass died in New Delhi from accidental electrocution. His parents took him to a clinic where the medical staff worked on the dead boy for two hours without success. After they gave up, a doctor told the parents to call a mortician, and the facility charged them 5,000 rupees (about $110). Rather than calling a mortician, they instead called a man named Rodrick at the nearby Deliverance Church, who then called one of his church staff members named Savitri. Savitri brought two other Christians to Arjun's home, and together they began praying over the dead body at about 10:00 pm. They prayed and prayed for the next six hours. Then at 4:00 am, Arjun suddenly sprang back to life! He showed no signs of brain damage or other physical problems except for a terrible scar behind his left ear where the electric wire hit.

James Rutz reported that he asked Savitri through an interpreter, "How many resurrections have you been involved with in the six years that you've been doing ministry?" "Sixteen," she said. Rutz went on to say, "For a moment my brain froze. Then I began to reevaluate my life. *[Who wouldn't?]* I would give you Savitri's email address so you could check her out for yourself, but she doesn't have one. She can't read."

Rutz also shared the following story.

> "A distinguished but modest friend of mine – I'll call him Larry – was invited by German evangelist Reinhard Bonnke to visit his tent crusade in Botswana is 1986. Seated on the platform with his wife, Mallory, looking out over the audience of 10,000, Larry was amazed to see numerous healings, including eight blind people who came forward and received their sight. The next day at lunch, Larry got to chat with Bonnke, who said, looking downcast, 'Gosh, Larry, I'm sorry you happened to come at such a low time. We only had eight blind people healed last night.'"

I also love the following account of Rutz's friend Barclay Tait, which verifies the "seer" anointing.

As Rutz tells it, Barclay Tait was sitting on a bench at the outlet mall in Gatlinburg, Tennessee in 1999 when three couples and two children clad in jeans and T-shirts walked by. Sensing something in his spirit, Barclay stood up and said, "How y'all doin' today? Which one of you is Eddie?" A short man hesitantly raised his hand. Barclay said, "Well, Eddie, God wants you to know that you made the right decision in your ministry. It was hard, but you did what the Lord wanted, and now He's going to bless you. So just ignore the folks who are criticizing you." The man started weeping. As I too have experienced, it's very touching when you learn by a close encounter that God knows your name, is moved by your cares and concerns, and loves you enough to send a special messenger to lift your spirits.

Here's yet another from Rutz' book that verifies the function and modern-day office of the prophet.

> "Because my friends Kay [male] and Julie Hiramine are well-known Christian leaders, they were invited to the big GCOWE convention is Seoul, Korea in 1995. At that time, Julie was pregnant with their first child, but she wasn't showing. Yet during the convention, seven women approached her at seven different times with the same three-point message: 'You're pregnant. You're going to have a girl. She's going to be a prophetess.' These women were from *seven* countries on four continents, and none of them knew Julie. Little Brianna arrived as promised, and sure enough, she has turned out to be a prophetess.

> "What the women in Seoul didn't mention was that Brianna was going to be a 'Strong-Willed Child' – the crown princess, in fact, of all strong-willed children. As a two-year old, she redefined 'feisty.' She has since mellowed, but without those messages in Seoul, Kay and Julie might have despaired or written off Brianna's prophecies at bratty, show-off behavior…or worse.

> "[Brianna's] very first prophecy came at 18 months! As you might imagine, her syntax wasn't too sophisticated. But the message was accurate: It confirmed that a young couple named Paul and

Nancy Rivas were to move from California to Colorado Springs for ministry there to work with Kay and Julie. The message, delivered at a rather high decibel level, was: 'PAUL AND NANCY! PAUL AND NANCY! *HERE! NOW*!!!' Paul and Nancy came."

Rutz also tells of the account of a missionary in Guatemala who read all of Isaiah 53 over and over to a circle of Indians mourning the death of a boy until he came back to life!

The *Midnight Herald* reported the story of Duad, Manu, and some other members of the Indian Pentecostal Church in Dunger, Northern India. After the death of a six-year-old boy, they simply prayed in Jesus' Name after placing their Bibles on the dead body, wherein the boy awakened!

Oh yes! The miraculous is alive and well!

Faith Sets the Stage for Miracles

You probably noticed that most of these accounts are of people in undeveloped nations. Why is that?

Let's consider that cessationism is primarily a Western mindset. Third World Christians typically are not cessationists because they see too many demonstrations of God's power to believe such a thing. Christians in developing nations have only God to rely on rather than sophisticated medical interventions and welfare programs. Their faith is in God's supply; thus, they see more demonstrations of His provision.

Most of the jaw-dropping sort of miracles are indeed happening in undeveloped nations where many people have nothing upon which to rely except God. Their faith is strong, probably because it *must* be. Or perhaps because they don't have as many distractions drawing their attention away from spiritual things compared to Western Christians. Or maybe it's because they have not intellectualized the Bible like Western Christians tend to, but rather take it on face value in child-like faith and see miracles as a result.

Unbelief is a roadblock to the miraculous, which explains why there isn't more of it in the Western Church. Even Jesus was stymied by the lack of faith among those in His hometown of Nazareth. Mark 6 explains that because of the unbelief in that town, Jesus could do no mighty miracles there except heal a few sick people (see Mark 6:1-6).

On another occasion, Jesus took a blind man by the hand and led him out of the faithless village of Bethsaida to get him healed. Bethsaida was a village Jesus later denounced for their stark unbelief. He declared,

> **"Woe to you, Chorazin! Woe to you, Bethsaida! For if the miracles that were performed in you had been performed in Tyre and Sidon, they would have repented long ago in sackcloth and ashes.**
> -Matthew 11:21

Because of Jesus' compassion for that blind man from Bethsaida, He led him out of that environment of unbelief before ministering to him. And even then, this was the only recorded time when Jesus had to minister to a person twice in order to get him healed. The most extraordinary manifestations of God's power are in environments of faith!

The most extraordinary manifestations of God's power are in environments of faith!

Is it any wonder, therefore, why American Christians don't see more of the power of God on display? Apparently, God doesn't have much to work with in the American Church in this regard.

We are like Bethsaida and Nazareth. We have too often narrowed down the Bible to a book of good stories teaching moral principles rather than a handbook for how to do life in Christ! We have rationalized why we aren't walking in signs and wonders with tidy little sterilizing explanations of why those things died out with the apostles and aren't for us today. Thus, we have been left with the neutered form of Christianity today in the West that rarely has enough power to cure a runny nose.

We have become like the Israelites of old, of whom the Scriptures say,

> *How often they provoked Him in the wilderness and grieved Him in the desert! Yes, again and again they tempted God, and LIMITED the Holy One of Israel.* -Psalm 78:40-41 (KJV, emphasis mine)

Unbelief limits God, and it grieves Him. Unbelief doesn't limit God because He is finite, but because He has chosen to restrict what He does to the prayers and faith of His people. The fact that God invites His people to partner with Him to advance His Kingdom on the earth is a concept that might take another entire book to unpackage. Suffice it to say, however, that this does explain, in part, why Western Christians tend to be so impotent as a whole and why Christians in undeveloped nations are walking in signs and wonders. It all comes down to faith.

Hebrews 11:1 explains that faith is the substance of things hoped for, the evidence of things not yet seen. Hebrews 11:6 tells us that without faith, it's impossible to please God.

Despite this troubling lack of faith in the Western Church, there is a glimmer of hope on the horizon. The prayers of saints hungry for God's Kingdom to come in full expression have hit His ears, and He is responding. And this is the basis for James Rutz's book, *Mega Shift*. As Rutz explains,

"Predominant power has suddenly shifted into the hands of us nobodies. Our big sleep has ended, our 1,700-year nightmare is over, and we are launching the final transformation of the Earth. A vast, cleansing storm is roaring toward us from abroad. This is the next step up from Protestantism, though the beliefs remain the same. It is a joyful mega shift away from pastor-centered, spectator religion toward a more Biblical Church where God works directly through *you* – and you are empowered to do wonders."

We have yet to see the full manifestation of this mega shift in the West, but I believe we will. The Five-Fold Ministry and Gifts of the Spirit are abundantly operative in churches where they are welcomed, and increasingly, miracles are accompanying them.

> *The Five-Fold Ministry and Gifts of the Spirit are abundantly operative in churches where they are welcomed, and increasingly, miracles are accompanying them.*

Yes, the explosion of Christianity globally is happening through continuationists! And it's coming to America! In fact, it's already here, but just in isolated pockets so far. But I believe we will see miraculous demonstrations of God's power become more widespread in the coming years. As the darkness threatens to cover the land, the light will become that much brighter!

Before I close this chapter, I must tell you about my friends, Mark and Juli Suverkrup. For years Juli and Mark tried to have a child without success. Eventually, fertility specialists told them they could not bear children, a report Juli refused to accept. Instead, she prayed in faith for a son, and felt impressed by the Holy Spirit to go to Genesis 30 and read the account of Rachel, who had been childless until the Lord opened her womb. Juli perceived God instructing her to declare Genesis 30:22-24 over herself and personalize it. Juli began declaring the following over herself every day, several times per day: *"Then God remembered Juli, and God listened to her and opened her womb. And she conceived and bore a son. And she called his name Joseph."*

In two months, Juli conceived and later gave birth to a healthy son, who they named Joseph. Today Joseph Suverkrup is a tall, handsome young professional.

But that's not the end of Juli's story. God is using Juli to help other women in similar circumstances develop their own faith for God to help them conceive. As Juli likes to playfully say, "God is using me to help dozens of women get pregnant!"

One such woman is my niece, Jodi Kolbe. Jodi and her husband, Jeff had been trying to have a baby for many years. Unfortunately, fertility treatments had not worked, and they were starting to give up hope. On the day they met, Juli prophesied over Jodi. "You will be pregnant by this time next year." And sure enough, she was! Jodi now has two beautiful children, Jennika and Jasper, who are the delight of my visits to Springfield, Missouri.

Yes, prophecy is still in full operation in God's Kingdom for those who believe. Healing is likewise part of the salvation package for those who choose to believe. Likewise with tongues and every other Spiritual Gift named in the Scriptures.

I'm happy the Christians in the first four centuries didn't believe that the miraculous passed away with the first apostles. History records that Rome, for example, was converted to Christianity in the fourth century primarily because of the power of God on display among the Christians. Emperor Constantine himself saw a vision of a cross in the sky, and later that night had a dream where Christ appeared to him.

The early Christians were not cessationsists! On the contrary, they proved that Spiritual Gifts, the offices of the Five-Fold Ministry, and the miraculous power of God are for every generation. And you can thank God for using faith-filled continuationists to blaze the trail of the most significant expansions of Christianity the world has ever seen, both past and present!

6

THE ROYAL LAW OF LOVE

"Of all the things God intends for us to be, He intends for us to be peacemakers."

-Smith Wigglesworth, the great early 20th century evangelist and faith healer

In the Introduction I briefly mentioned the importance approaching these peripheral doctrinal issues with the goal of maintaining unity in the Body of Christ. It is therefore fitting that we end on the same note and elaborate on the importance of this chief aim among the saints.

Why God Hates Division

There is a troubling trend I have observed on social media. I have seen videos posted by people I will call the "Bible Police" attacking other sincere followers of Christ. With clickbait titles such as, "I can't believe he said THIS!", these self-proclaimed purveyors of Bible doctrine will call out a particular group, theological camp, or person and denounce them for false doctrine for all the internet world to see. Even the salvation of those being targeted is called into question. Often these "heresy hunters" lift a sentence or two out of context to misrepresent the person or group. And it all sounds so convincing as long as you're hearing only one side of the argument.

The book of Proverbs provides some brilliant yet simple wisdom along these lines.

> **The first to state his case seems right until another comes and cross-examines him.** -Proverbs 18:17

Most often, however, people will not do the due diligence of looking at both sides of an issue or argument with equal attention. *Who has time for that?* Instead, people will read a meme on Facebook or see a 10-minute video on YouTube or a 1-minute video on Tik Tok and then feel as though they have a highly developed theology, responding with prideful disdain toward those who do not share their newly developed ideas. In some cases, this can negatively impact relationships and the trajectory of people's spiritual development.

For example, people may begin very well in terms of their walk with the Lord as they get planted in a church where they are growing and loving the fellowship, feeding on the Word of God, delighting in God's presence, and showing the fruits of the Spirit. But that's when Satan gets them in his crosshairs. As with any brilliant tactician, Satan will not allow a dramatic growth trajectory to continue unchallenged.

> *As with any brilliant tactician, Satan will not allow a dramatic growth trajectory to continue unchallenged.*

These satanic counter measures are why the Apostle Peter instructed Christ followers to be aware. He said in First Peter 5:8,

Be sober-minded and alert. Your adversary the devil prowls around like a roaring lion, seeking someone to devour.

Satan often entices susceptible churchgoers in whom he has been given a foothold to sow seeds of doubt and discord in the unsuspecting. This demonic influence is compounded by the divisive books, disdainful documentaries, and hurtful videos some parties produce. These can sour people on the ministries where they have come to know the Lord and grown exponentially under godly and loving leadership. Eventually, this causes some to disconnect from the garden where God has carefully and sovereignly planted them.

Mission accomplished. When people divide themselves over doctrinal issues like this, it's evidence that Satan's tactics worked in their case. As well intentioned they may be, these "Bible Police" and "guardians of truth" aren't helping anything when they cause this kind of division in the Body of Christ. Even some videos I have watched with some degree of substance to them are presented in such condescending and condemning tones that I am grieved. I know the Holy Spirit must be grieved as well.

Allow me to make a plea to social media warriors. Gentlemen and ladies, if you feel you must call out someone for false doctrine, please keep two things in mind.

First, be cordial because the world is watching and taking note. There is no place in the lives of Christians for vitriolic attacks against one another or even subtly condescending tones. Proverbs 16:21 says that **the sweetness of one's speech promotes instruction.** Make your words sweet, because you never know when you will have to eat them, which leads to my next point.

Secondly, you never know; you might be the one in the wrong. The beliefs and doctrines of God's people often do change and develop over time. For example, I used to have intense negative feelings about speaking in tongues, but I changed my mind as I investigated God's Word and historical evidence more deeply.

I recently saw a YouTube video by someone who admitted to being wrong about tongues in his past videos. Therefore, you will save face by making your words gracious if someone happens to prove you wrong and you end up doing an about-face. I believe Trueblood's Maxim is good food for thought to help guide us:

> "He who begins with loving his own view of truth more than the truth itself, will end in loving his own denomination more than Christ, and ultimately loving himself most of all."

I agree with Pastor Jack Hayford on this point when he wrote in his book, *A Passion for Fullness*,

> "Jesus is stepping into the middle of His disciples' arguments. To those ready to call fire down on their apparent enemies, He is still saying, 'You know not of what spirit you are.'"

I'm not suggesting, on the other hand, that there's never a time to call out heresy and apostasy. I'm calling out some heretical practices right now, in fact. Unfortunately, I have found that what some people are calling heresy is nothing more than their own superficial interpretation of the Scriptures. I'm not against people being on their own journey of faith and learning as they go. But I *am* saddened when people proceed to cause great damage and division in the Body of Christ by vilifying others with whom they disagree, which in some cases causes the babes in Christ to fall out of fellowship with people whom they were experiencing great spiritual growth and fruitfulness.

The Word of God tells us that one of the seven things God hates, which are indeed an abomination to Him, is when people sow discord among the brethren (see Proverbs 6:16-19). And the resulting relational fallout is one of the reasons God hates it because it divides His Body, damages churches, causes love to turn cold, and harms people spiritually and emotionally.

Brethren, if a person is causing division among the members of the Body, he or she cannot be operating with the Spirit of God. That sort of thing is hellish. What some people call wise and spiritual is, in fact, demonic. The book of James speaks to this.

> **13Who is wise and understanding among you? Let him show it by his good conduct, by deeds done in the humility that comes from wisdom. 14But if you harbor bitter jealousy and selfish ambition in your hearts, do not boast in it or deny the truth. 15Such wisdom does not come from above, but is earthly, unspiritual, demonic. -James 3:13-15**

Learning to Live in Unity While Disagreeing on Peripheral Matters

Regardless of what theological camp or denomination with which you identify, each of us who name the Name of Jesus Christ are obligated to abide by the laws of love and unity. To this end, the Apostle Paul addressed the factions in his day with a beautiful discourse in Romans chapter 14. I urge you to read that passage after you put down this book. Paul begins the chapter in verse 1 by instructing us to **Accept him whose faith is weak, without passing judgment on his opinions.**

People who believe in Gifts of the Spirit may believe the faith of one who doesn't is weak, and vice versa. Nevertheless, we must accept one another without judgment.

Paul continues his treatise by addressing factions between people who observe various food restrictions and those who eat anything, as well as those who observe various holy days versus those who believe every day is the same before God. Paul's message was that each person does what he does to honor God. Perhaps a particular position does indeed lack knowledge, but that's beside the point according to Romans 14. If a person observes certain holy days, for example, he does it from a heart desiring to please God. And if a person maintains the conviction that all days are the same, he too does it yearning to please God. This is also true of the person who refrains from eating certain foods and the person who eats everything with thanksgiving. They both do it with a desire to please God. Therefore, Paul instructs,

> *3The one who eats everything must not belittle the one who does not, and the one who does not eat everything must not judge the one who does, for God has accepted him. 4Who are you to judge someone else's servant? To his own master he stands or falls. And he will stand, for the Lord is able to make him stand.*

Paul doesn't stop there. As if to drive home the point with jackhammer-like force and repetition, he continues.

> *10Why, then, do you judge your brother? Or why do you belittle your brother? For we will all stand before God's judgment seat. 11It is written: "As surely as I live, says the Lord, every knee will bow before Me; every tongue will confess to God." 12So then, each of us will give an account of himself to God. 13Therefore let us stop judging one another... 19So then, let us pursue what leads to peace and to mutual edification.*

At this point, we can sit back and breathe a sigh of relief that the Holy Spirit, through Paul, is done pointing out our arrogant judgments of one another in his discourse. Aah! Not so fast! Paul has not laid down his jackhammer just yet. The life-giving instruction continues in chapter 15.

> **¹We who are strong ought to bear with the shortcomings of the weak and not to please ourselves. ²Each of us should please his neighbor for his good, to build him up. ³For even Christ did not please Himself... ⁵Now may the God who gives endurance and encouragement grant you harmony with one another in Christ Jesus, ⁶so that with one mind and one voice you may glorify the God and Father of our Lord Jesus Christ. ⁷Accept one another, then, just as Christ accepted you, in order to bring glory to God.**

Therefore, God's Kingdom is not even about who speaks in tongues and who doesn't, who prophesies or doesn't. Jesus prayed in John 17 that His followers would be one just as the Father and Son are one. In fact, Jesus referred to this unity *five times* in His prayer! Unity among the saints is very important to Jesus!

Satan is a highly organized strategist, and one of the most effective tactics he uses is *"divide and conquer."* Division is a sign of satanic influence, but unity is a sign of submission to Christ! If we have given in to Satan's divisive suggestions and distanced ourselves from our brethren on the grounds of peripheral doctrinal disagreements, then we have been seduced by a dark spirit of pride and division, and God cannot fully bless those who operate

Division is a sign of satanic influence, but unity is a sign of submission to Christ!

this way. **God *resists the proud,* but gives *grace to humble,*** the Bible says in various places.

I should clarify that this unity is for those who are *genuinely* in the faith and endeavoring to please God to the best of their ability according to the Word of God. We should not feel obligated to align ourselves with people who purposefully twist, ignore, or manipulate the Scriptures for their own sinful and selfish desires. The Bible even tells us in various places to be cautious about fellowshipping with such people at all. But those are not the people to whom this writing is aimed. It is intended for people who earnestly love God, honor His Word, and esteem the Church.

"Tell us how you *really* feel about it?"

Every so often, I have heard someone communicate his or her opinion about something in a very forceful way, and a bystander replies, "Tell us how you *really* feel about it." The playful remark is a lighthearted way to say, "You really have strong feelings about that, don't you?!"

Similarly, it is fitting to communicate the strength and force with which God chose to convey His feelings about His Church walking in love and unity in the famous "love chapter" in First Corinthians 13. Verse 1 says, ***If I speak in the tongues of men and of angels, but have not love, I have become a sounding brass or a clanging cymbal.***

The King James version describes the cymbals as "tinkling." This instruction becomes even more significant when one considers the context. The Apostle Paul was writing to the Corinthian Christians. Corinth was a culture steeped in ritualistic paganism and sexual perversion. Much of the society worshiped a goddess they named Aphrodite, the so-called goddess of love. The worship of Aphrodite included prostitution at the temple erected in her honor. Every woman of every family and social standing who worshiped Aphrodite was expected to take a turn periodically serving as a temple prostitute. During their service, temple prostitutes would cut their hair short and put little bells and cymbals around their ankles and wrists as an indication they were on duty and available.

The gravitas of Paul's words becomes even more impactful when considering this cultural context. When people read "sounding brass" and "tinkling cymbals," they immediately made the intended connection and drew a vivid mental image of temple prostitutes. In so many words, Paul was saying that people claiming to be Christ's followers but who do not walk in love and unity toward one another are no better than pagan whores! *That's how strongly the Spirit of God wanted to communicate this truth.*

The epistle of John advanced this concept further by calling into question the salvation of those who show contempt for their brethren in Christ. He wrote in First John 4:29 that **anyone who does not love his brother, whom he has seen, cannot love God, whom he has not seen.**

Brothers and sisters, we cannot afford to miss this point. Our salvation may hang in the balance. The merit of our witness for Christ *unquestionably* hangs in the balance, as does the advancement and fruitfulness of God's Kingdom through His Church. The division that marks the Body of Christ today is one of the reasons we have not been more effective in reaching our culture. Elitist sectarianism is one of the saddest trends occurring in the Church today. Many Christians who are so quick to denounce racism, and rightly so, will nevertheless do an about-face regarding other Christians who do not share their theological dogmas. This is true on both sides of the debate addressed in this book, and in nearly all denominational dividing lines. We naturally gravitate toward our favorite "flavors" regarding church styles and methodologies while unconsciously believing we are more enlightened for choosing our favorite flavors. Then we accuse others of religious snobbery for doing the same. And a watching world responds by dismissing us as irrelevant.

The need for greater effectiveness in reaching the culture for Christ is the reason for establishing the First International Congress on World Evangelism, also known as the Lausanne Congress, held in Lausanne, Switzerland in 1974. Called by a committee headed by Billy Graham, the Congress was a conference of some 2,700 evangelical Christian leaders from 150 nations who gathered to discuss the progress, resources, and methods of evangelizing the world. The Lausanne Congress made a bold declaration regarding the ministry of the Holy Spirit, calling upon Christians of all doctrinal persuasions to unite in praying that God's Church would become more effective in reaching the world through *all* the demonstrations of His Holy Spirit. In speaking for so diverse a group of evangelicals, the declaration of the Congress was unlike any such statement before, including these words from Article 14:

> "We therefore call upon all Christians to pray for such a visitation of the sovereign Spirit of God that *all* His fruit may appear in *all* His people and that *all* His Gifts may enrich the Body of Christ. *Only then* will the whole Church become a fit instrument in His hands, that the whole earth may hear His voice."

Amen! Doesn't your spirit resonate with that declaration? May the love of God, therefore, guide us and unite us in perfect harmony, that His people may display His splendor in the earth in all its fullness.

I pray this discussion has stirred you to study the Scriptures for yourself rather than taking someone else's word for it. The Bible tells us in Second Timothy 2:15, ***"study to show thyself approved,*** *a workman who needeth not to be ashamed, rightly dividing the Word of truth."* (KJV)

In the final analysis, let us in the Church be people who not only endeavor to approach the Word humbly in how it might speak to us, but also strive to heed the instructions of Scripture to *"make every effort to keep the unity of the Spirit through the bond of peace"* (Ephesians 4:3).

EPILOGUE

_____

UNDERSTANDING AND RECEIVING
THE BAPTISM OF THE HOLY SPIRIT

In Hebrews 6, we are given a brief list of fundamental biblical doctrines maturing Christians are expected to master.

> *¹Therefore let us leave the elementary teachings about Christ and go on to maturity, not laying again the foundation of repentance from dead works, and of faith in God, ²instruction about baptisms, the laying on of hands, the resurrection of the dead, and eternal judgment. ³And this we will do, if God permits.* -Hebrews 6:1-3

Note the doctrine of "baptisms" in verse 2 is plural. There is more than one baptism. In fact, there are *three*. The first baptism is our baptism into Christ when we first believed.

> *For in one Spirit we were all baptized into one body, whether Jews or Greeks, slave or free, and we were all given one Spirit to drink.* -1 Corinthians 12:13

⁴There is one body and one Spirit, just as you were called to one hope when you were called; ⁵one Lord, one faith, one baptism... -Ephesians 4:4-5

The second baptism is performed by the hands of people and refers to water baptism, a symbolic ceremony representing the death of our old life and the resurrection into the new.

Therefore, go and make disciples of all nations, baptizing them in the name of the Father, and of the Son, and of the Holy Spirit... -Matthew 28:19

We were therefore buried with Him through baptism into death, in order that, just as Christ was raised from the dead through the glory of the Father, we too may walk in newness of life. -Romans 6:4

The third baptism is the Baptism of the Holy Spirit with the evidence of speaking in tongues and is referenced by Jesus after His resurrection.

"For John truly baptized with water, but you shall be baptized with the Holy Spirit not many days from now." -Acts 1:5

This third baptism is not required for salvation. However, it appears to necessary for walking in a new dimension of power and a greater level of fruitfulness in Christ's Kingdom.

For instance, the Baptism of the Holy Spirit with the evidence of speaking in tongues appears to be one of the most important tools for living in the supernatural. I don't know a single person who operates in signs and wonders who *doesn't* speak in tongues. Maybe a few do, but I haven't met them. The two seem to go hand-in-hand. Conversely, people who reject tongues also typically deny that God still does miracles today.

One benefit we can expect from this third baptism is an enhanced boldness in sharing one's faith, as Jesus promised in Acts 1:8.

> **"But you will receive power when the Holy Spirit comes on you; and you will be my witnesses in Jerusalem, and in all Judea and Samaria, and to the ends of the earth."**

This promise is speaking of a special endowment of power that would enable the first disciples to be powerful witnesses for Christ. Remember, even though they already belonged to Christ, this endowment of power had yet to be experienced. After Jesus' death on the cross, the disciples had cowered in hiding, afraid of the authorities. Not long after that, however, they *all* received the Baptism of the Holy Spirit with the evidence of speaking in tongues on the day of the celebration of Pentecost, and immediately afterward, they began boldly proclaiming the message of Christ publicly. As a result of Peter's very first public address that day, 3,000 people received Christ (see Acts 2:40-41). And it wasn't only Peter's message that resulted in that response. A miraculous sign paved the way just before Peter stood to speak.

What was that miraculous sign? It was the sign of all the believers being in one accord and all speaking in tongues (Acts 2:4). Some would undoubtedly argue that the tongues mentioned in Acts 2 was not gibberish no one could understand, but, in fact, those speaking were understood by over a dozen different dialects (v. 6-11). This is gloriously true. But rather than disproving the validity of the modern-day practice of tongues, this actually represents one of the *different kinds* of tongues. This kind of tongues is a form where people speak one language, but bystanders hear in their own language! This was a powerful miracle, and First Corinthians 14:22 says this kind of tongues is a sign to unbelievers.

Other forms of tongues are mentioned in the Bible as well, such as the kind used to bring a revelation from God to the church through tongues and interpretation of tongues (1 Corinthians 14:13, 27-28).

Another form is a "prayer language," as it has been called, which is the ability to pray in tongues for one's own edification (1 Corinthians 14:4, 14-15, Jude 1:20). This kind of praying is also referred to in Romans 8:26.

> **Now likewise also, the Spirit joins to help us in weakness; for we do not know the things which we should pray for as it behooves, but the Spirit Himself makes intercession with inexpressible groanings.** (BLB)

This form of praying in the Spirit is almost reflexive during times of stress or anguish. For example, in the summer of 2021 my youngest child, Drew, who was 15 at the time, got into some serious trouble when it was discovered that some of the boys he had become friends with on his homeschool basketball team were making some terrible choices, and they had drawn Drew into their sinful behavior. At first, Drew was remorseful only because he was in so much trouble. But I began bombarding heaven, praying in tongues for an hour a day for him for five days straight. The following Sunday, we had a guest speaker at our church who preached about "rending our hearts." At the end of the service, during the altar call, Drew was up front, face down on the carpet, sobbing and heaving, snot and all! It was one of the most dramatic scenes of repentance I have ever witnessed. He has been different ever since. When I catch Drew in the act of something now, he's usually praying! Hallelujah!!

Hence, praying in tongues can be a potent tool in your spiritual arsenal. When you don't know what to pray, the Holy Spirit takes over and prays the perfect prayer, more powerful than you could pray on your own!

A new dimension of operating in the supernatural can also be expected as another benefit of the Baptism in the Holy Spirit. Many Christians have testified to having experienced new liberty over sinful habits, release from inner bondages and inhibitions, and freedom from addictions. There is also an overflow of joy and peace, a stronger sense of the presence of God, and even a clearer understanding of the Word of God.

Internationally known minister Andrew Wommack recalls an experience with a man highly educated in the Bible. This gentleman was seminary trained but had not experienced the Baptism of the Holy Spirit. This man expressed great frustration regarding Andrew Wommack's deep insight in the Scriptures without being formally trained. Andrew Wommack attributes his knowledge and insight into the Word of God to the Baptism of the Holy Spirit.

Andrew Wommack's experience with that man is reminiscent of how the Pharisees and Sadducees, who were highly educated in the Old Testament, expressed dismay at the knowledge and insight of Jesus, who had no formal training. Matthew 3:16 tells us that after Jesus had been water baptized, the Holy Spirit descended upon Him like a dove. It was shortly after when the Holy Spirit led Jesus into the wilderness to fast, and then His ministry began with great signs and wonders.

Yet another benefit to expect with the Baptism of the Holy Spirit is an enhanced sense of love toward others, especially those in the faith. This is demonstrated quite clearly in the early Church in the book of Acts.

> *[44]All the believers were together and had everything in common. [45]Selling their possessions and goods, they shared with anyone who was in need. [46]With one accord they continued to meet daily in the temple courts and to break bread from house to house, sharing their meals with gladness and sincerity of heart, [47]praising God and enjoying the favor of all the people.* -Acts 2:44-47

This harmonious unity and sharing had not previously been the case with the disciples. Even as they walked with Jesus, there were power plays and bickering as to which one was the greatest. On one occasion, when James and John petitioned through their mother to sit on Jesus' left and right when He came into His reign, the Scriptures say the other disciples were "indignant" with them (see Matthew 20:20-24). On another occasion, the two brothers wanted to call down fire on a Samaritan village (see Luke 9:54), and there are other instances of the disciples being less than loving toward others. But all that changed after the Baptism of the Holy Spirit.

Similarly, it has been an interesting point to ponder that those I have seen and heard denounce the Gifts of the Spirit and the Five-Fold Ministry typically do it with very critical spirits, harsh judgments, and divisive methods. I see no such behavior among those Baptized in the Holy Spirit, however. That has been *my* experience, at least. Those targeted on social media, books, and sermons typically give no response at all, or if they do, the responses I have seen are very gracious. I find that to be telling.

Doesn't Every Christian Already Have the Holy Spirit?

To clarify, *all* who have called on Jesus for salvation have been given the gift of the indwelling Holy Spirit. Jesus conferred the Holy Spirit upon His disciples after His resurrection, signifying their participation in the gift of salvation.

> [21]*Again Jesus said to them, "Peace be with you. As the Father has sent Me, so also I am sending you."* [22]*When He had said this, He breathed on them and said, "Receive the Holy Spirit."* -John 20:21-22

The imagery there is *breath*. Jesus breathed on them – He exhaled. We don't know whether that was the literal mechanism that filled them, but the symbolism is undoubtedly there, and they *did* receive the Holy Spirit as an initial infilling for salvation.

The Holy Spirit's role in the redemptive experience is the title deed of one's salvation. Ephesians 4:30 says the Holy Spirit is the Father's seal on His beloved for the day of redemption. The Holy Spirit is described in God's Word as our Comforter (John 14:26), Counselor (John 15:26), and Guide (John 16:13). Jesus said the Holy Spirit convicts of sin (John 16:8), leads us into all truth (John 16:13a), and even shows us things to come (John 16:13b).

These are all amazing benefits of having a relationship with Jesus Christ. However, what Jesus did for His disciples, as recorded in John 20:21-22 is different than the *Baptism* of the Holy Spirit. If this experience was the same as the Baptism of the Holy Spirit, there was no reason for those disciples, who had already received the Holy Spirit from Jesus, to wait for the Holy Spirit to come upon them in the Upper Room. Remember, Jesus also told them,

"For John truly baptized with water, but you shall be baptized with the Holy Spirit not many days from now." ... But you will receive power when the Holy Spirit comes on you; and you will be my witnesses in Jerusalem, and in all Judea and Samaria, and to the ends of the earth." -Acts 1:5,8

When Jesus made this promise, the disciples had not yet been emboldened with the Holy Spirit's power. As already stated, recall that after Jesus' crucifixion, the disciples cowered in hiding in fear of the authorities. When they received the Baptism of the Holy Spirit on the day of Pentecost, however, they came out of hiding and began boldly proclaiming the gospel. The Baptism of the Holy Spirit empowered them for service.

Thus, there is another level of the Holy Spirit's activity in the life of the Christian, and this next level is called the Baptism of the Holy Spirit.

Receiving the Baptism of the Holy Spirit: Are you Ready?

If you have read this far, perhaps you are ready to take the leap and invite God to baptize you with the Holy Spirit and fire.

Although there is no formula for receiving the Baptism of the Holy Spirit, there are a few things to keep in mind.

First, there must be an attitude of repentance.

Repent, then, and turn to God, so that your sins may be wiped out, that times of refreshing may come from the Lord, and that He may send the Messiah, who has been appointed for you—even Jesus.
-Acts 3:19-20 (NIV)

Repentance isn't simply a one-time act when a person first responds to the Lord. Repentance is a lifestyle which leads the follower of Christ to make adjustments daily. Even the Christian can be harboring areas of unrepentant sin, and the Holy Spirit – or the Spirit of Holiness – is most at home in a vessel consecrated to Him through a lifestyle of holiness. We should therefore repent of any areas of known sin as we seek a deeper infilling of the Holy Spirit. After that, the Holy Spirit will do the rest, taking His cleansing work in the child of God even deeper.

The second thing to remember in receiving the Baptism of the Holy Spirit is simply seeking and asking. This Baptism is not automatically received as a benefit of salvation; it must be asked for and received by faith, just like salvation.

> *⁹So I tell you: Ask, and it will be given to you; seek, and you will find; knock, and the door will be opened to you. ¹⁰For everyone who asks receives; he who seeks finds; and to him who knocks, the door will be opened. ¹¹What father among you, if his son asks for a fish, will give him a snake instead? ¹²Or if he asks for an egg, will give him a scorpion? ¹³So if you who are evil know how to give good gifts to your children, how much more will your Father in heaven give the Holy Spirit to those who ask Him!" -Luke 13:9-13*

The Father delights in giving His Holy Spirit in a measure beyond the initial salvation experience. However, when a person asks for the Baptism of the Holy Spirit, the receiving part must be done *by faith*. Some people are waiting for God to zap them and make them start speaking in tongues, but it doesn't always work that way. It's probably rarer when it happens this way. Most often, people have to *participate* with the Holy Spirit. Then, when they ask for the Baptism of the Holy Spirit, they must believe God has heard them and responded. The basis for this is the previously mentioned passage in Luke 11. We must believe that when we ask, God delights in us like earthly fathers delight in their children, and God knows how to give generously. Let's look at a portion of that passage again.

> ¹¹**What father among you, if his son asks for a fish, will give him a snake instead? ¹²Or if he asks for an egg, will give him a scorpion? ¹³So if you who are evil know how to give good gifts to your children, how much more will your Father in heaven give the Holy Spirit to those who ask Him!"**

This is God's promise to us. You must trust that God will not fail to back His Word. When you ask and receive by faith, God is going to respond.

Receiving by faith is not where it ends, however. Faith requires action. You must then cooperate with the Holy Spirit by moving your mouth. The Holy Spirit will begin welling up in you, and those strange syllables coming to your mind must be given utterance! This is how it works. And it may or may not come with ecstatic emotions. Emotions do often accompany this experience, but not always. Emotions have very little to do with responding in faith, in fact. As you respond in faith and simply speak out whatever syllables or sounds come to your heart and mind, the Holy Spirit will respond by giving you more. That's how your prayer language is developed.

I know many people who experienced the Baptism of the Holy Spirit who received it in a dramatic, emotional fashion, such as the man in our church mentioned earlier who began speaking in tongues after a demon was cast out of him. Many others,

Emotions have very little to do with responding in faith.

however, received this Gift very differently, simply by responding in faith without any accompanying emotions or spiritual fireworks. I am one of those people.

My prayer language developed slowly over several months, a few words at a time; until now I can pray in tongues at length. I had to bypass my intellect to get there, but this is not always a bad thing. God gave us brains for a reason, and He wants us to use them, but our intellects have their limits. In order to discern and experience the things of God's Kingdom, often we will have to set our intellects aside and respond in faith.

Because my prayer language developed without any spiritual fireworks, I often have wrestled with doubts about the legitimacy of my experience, thinking I may have conjured the whole thing up on my own. However, please again consider our passage in Luke 11. If a person asks for the Baptism of the Holy Spirit, God knows how to respond in kind. He is not going to give you a fake Baptism. Once again, it's a matter of walking by faith and not by sight (2 Corinthians 5:7).

In seeking God for the Baptism of the Holy Spirit, it is also helpful to have a man or woman of God assist you in prayer with the laying on of hands. The laying on of hands is taught throughout the Old and New Testaments as a method of impartation from one person to another. A seasoned man or woman of God who believes in and practices the Gifts of the Spirit can be very beneficial along these lines in helping you receive.

Even with the aforementioned concepts in mind, however, let's again consider that there is no formula for receiving the Baptism of the Holy Spirit. How one person receives may be very different than the next. The experience can be as individualized as salvation itself.

Words of Caution

Once you receive this special impartation, guard against getting puffed up with spiritual pride, as if you have "arrived" spiritually.

One of the benefits of the Baptism of the Holy Spirit, if truly experienced, is that it raises awareness of one's frailty. That heightened awareness thus increases the sense of need for a deeper work of God in one's life. It should never lead to smugness or pride.

> *One of the benefits of the Baptism of the Holy Spirit, if truly experienced, is that it causes a person to have a deeper sense of one's own frailty and thus an increased sense of need for a deeper work of God in one's life.*

The Word says Jesus will baptize us with the Holy Spirit and "fire" (see Matthew 3:11). This *fire* could be related to a refining fire. Malachi 3:3 tells us that God will come like a refiner of silver, burning away the dross. This is a picture of inner cleansing. There are definitely benefits to being baptized in the Holy Spirit and fire, but don't ever use that experience to be pretentious toward others who have not received it. It is a spiritual tool, and you did nothing to earn it.

The second word of caution is that **the Baptism of the Holy Spirit won't do much if you don't exercise it**. For a long time, I felt that my experience of being Baptized in the Holy Spirit had not resulted in much power, but I realized later this was because I wasn't exercising it much. For years, I hardly ever prayed in tongues. It wasn't until I began exercising this Gift in my private prayer time regularly that I truly began to see results in my personal life and ministry. It is through the exercising of this Gift, plus fasting regularly, that I began to see demonstrative authority over demons, the Holy Spirit using me to speak prophetically at times, and more victory in my personal life.

The Beauty of Spiritual Language

Finally, I want to share a story from Jack Hayfords' book, *The Beauty of Spiritual Language*. The late Jack Hayford was a very quiet, reserved, and cerebral pastor not given to emotion, and his experience spoke to me. I hope it encourages you as well.

Hayford tells of a flight he was on where he struck up a conversation with a man seated next to him. During their conversation, he learned this man had been highly trained in the languages of many ancient cultures. While they chatted, he felt the Holy Spirit prompt him. "Speak to him in tongues." Hayford understandably wrestled with the command. He wasn't sure he understood correctly, but after a few moments, he got an idea.

Hayford told the man he knew a few words in a foreign language, and didn't know what they meant, so he asked if he could speak those words to him to see if he could decipher them. The man eagerly agreed. Hayford then began to simply speak in tongues – utterances inspired by the Holy Spirit as he gave place to the Spirit's promptings. After a few brief moments of speaking to the man in tongues, Hayford stopped and waited for a response. The man sat there dumbfounded for a moment and then said, "Where did you learn those words? That language has been dead for centuries!"

Pastor Hayford responded by admitting he was speaking in tongues as the Spirit of God gave him utterance. Then he asked the man if he knew what the words meant. The man replied that he was speaking about the glorious love and works of God.

In this instance, the Gift of tongues was a sign to the unbelieving, similar to the scene in Acts 2 on the Day of Pentecost. Let that story encourage you that the Gift of tongues is an authentic Gift of the Spirit and is still in operation today, as are the other Spiritual Gifts and the offices of the Five-Fold Ministry.

You need not be afraid of the Gifts of the Spirit. God will never offer anything detrimental to your spiritual development. He loves you and wants to see you flourish in Christ. Therefore, every Gift He offers is in place for your enrichment. As His Word says in James 1:17, *Every good and perfect gift is from above, coming down from the Father of the heavenly lights, with whom there is no change or shifting shadow.*

If you need prayer or ministry, contact us at BlessedLifeFellowship.org or AndrewRobbinsMinistries.org. God bless you!

Other resources from Andrew Robbins can be accessed at
AndrewRobbinsMinistries.org.

OTHER HELPFUL RESOURCES

Book: *AWAKENED BY THE SPIRIT: Reclaiming the Forgotten Gift of God,* by Ron M. Phillips

Book: *A PASSION FOR FULLNESS: Don't let fear, doctrinal narrowness or spiritual smugness get in the way of a full experience of God,* by Jack Hayford

Book: *THE BEAUTY OF SPIRITUAL LANGUAGE: Unveiling the Mysteries of Speaking in Tongues,* by Jack Hayford

Podcast: *THE REVIVAL LIFESTYLE,* by Isaiah Saldivar. (See also Isaiah Saldivar's YouTube channel)

Ministry Website: *VLADIMIR SAVCHUCK MINISTRIES,* PastorVlad.org.

Book: *THEY SPEAK WITH OTHER TONGUES,* by John L. Sherrill.

Book: *UNLOCKING THE MYSTERIES OF THE HOLY SPRIT,* by Dr. Larry Ollison

Book: *THE HOLY SPIRIT: An Introduction,* by John Bevere

Book: *MEGA SHIFT: Igniting Spiritual Power,* by James Rutz

Ministry Website: *RICK RENNER MINISTRIES,* Renner.org.
- Video chats on the Baptism of the Holy Spirit - https://renner.org/topics/holy-spirit/
- Other books and resources on the Holy Spirit - https://renner.org/product-category/holy-spirit/

Printed in the United States
by Baker & Taylor Publisher Services